REMARKABLE
Resilience

The Life and
Legacy of
NOÉMI BAN
Beyond the
Holocaust

Diane M. Sue, Ph.D.

Published by Resilience Publishing
in partnership with Influence Publishing Inc., May 2022
ISBN: 979-8-9859273-0-6

Developmental Editing: Michael Fragnito
Copyediting: Candace Johnson
Proofreading: Lee Robinson
Front Cover Artwork: Sonya Shannon, www.sonya-shannon.com
Typesetting and Cover Design: Tara Eymundson

DISCLAIMER: Readers of this publication agree that neither Diane M. Sue, nor her publisher will be held responsible or liable for damages that may be alleged as resulting directly or indirectly from the use of this publication. Neither the publisher nor the author can be held accountable for the information provided by, or actions resulting from, accessing these resources.

CONTENT WARNING: This book contains descriptions of the Holocaust that may be distressing to some readers.

Dedication

For my dear friend, Noémi Ban, who dedicated her elder years to sharing her vision of a loving and peaceful world.

Testimonials

"Dr. Diane Sue is eminently qualified to bring Noémi's story to life. Not only did she and Noémi share decades of close friendship, Diane's academic and professional background have provided her with the skills to listen deeply and to eloquently describe Noémi's journey of transforming trauma into compassion and healing."

Ray Wolpow, Ph.D.

Professor Emeritus and former Director of the
Northwest Center for Holocaust, Genocide and Ethnocide Education,
Western Washington University

"A book filled with wisdom, compassion, and understanding, Noémi's story of survival against all odds is a powerful addition to Holocaust literature."

Malcolm Stern

Author of *Slay Your Dragons with Compassion*

"Noémi Ban is an inspiration to us all. This is a book that will inspire you. It must be read."

Eva Schloss

Author of *Eva's Story: A Survivor's Tale by the Stepsister of Anne Frank*

"I had the great privilege of knowing Noémi, and this important and beautiful book captures the essence of the Noémi I knew—her courage, kindness, and powerful presence. *Remarkable Resilience* is full of the inspiration and hope our world so desperately needs."

Karen Molenaar Terrell
Teacher and Author

"Noémi's wisdom about the importance of embracing love rather than hate has changed many lives, including mine. This book brings Noémi's grace, gentility, compassion, and forgiveness into clear focus. Her words are a beacon of light that inject hope, courage, determination, and spiritual resilience deep into the soul."

Joy Gilfilen
President of the Restorative Community Coalition,
Host of *iChange Justice* podcast

"This book demonstrates how resilience is formed through familial love and is strengthened within the self, and by friends, through the energy of love. Dr. Sue has rendered Noémi's words with palpable affection, expertise, and astuteness. Readers dealing with trauma and hard times will find that this book provides hope and inspiration."

Sarah Gillen
LMFT; Trauma and Family Therapist; Author of *From Hurt to Joy: How to Transform Self-Defeating Patterns with Energy Dynamics*

Contents

Acknowledgments

First and foremost, I thank my dear friend, Noémi Ban, for putting her trust in me and allowing me the incredible privilege of writing her life story. In addition to Noémi's engaging first-person accounts and vivid recollections, Noémi's sons, Dr. Steven Ban and George Ban, generously delved into childhood memories to fill in details about their escape from Hungary and immigration to the United States, and shared a memoir written in Hebrew by Noémi's father, Samu, as well as a diary in which Samu described searching for his family in the final months of World War II—a tear-stained memento that Noémi painstakingly translated from Hungarian to English, writing each page by hand just as her father had done decades earlier.

I was also fortunate to have access to newspaper articles about Noémi and videotaped interviews she completed over the years, as well as her youth-focused Holocaust memoir, *Sharing is Healing*, written with the assistance of Dr. Ray Wolpow from Western Washington University. I will be forever grateful to Dr. Wolpow, who generously allowed me access to the invaluable recordings, field notes, and photographs he compiled during Noémi's first return visit to Auschwitz and who patiently answered my queries about his experiences accompanying Noémi on this journey. Dr. Wolpow also allowed me to draw from his powerful doctoral dissertation, *Trauma, Literacy and the Pedagogy of Hope*, which includes insightful conversations with Noémi concerning her philosophy of education. I am also grateful to Professor Jim Lortz, a close friend of Noémi and producer of the documentary *My Name is Noémi*, for his insight and observations. My gratitude also goes to Dr. Fritz Brinkmann-Frisch, historian at the Documentation and Information Center located in Stadtallendorf, Germany, who shared information and generously responded to my queries related to the one thousand Hungarian women held prisoner in the Münchmühle sub-camp of the Buchenwald concentration camp.

I am immensely grateful for the encouragement of my developmental editor, Michael Fragnito, and, more recently, the heartfelt guidance from Julie Ann Salisbury, founder of Influence Publishing. I also appreciate the dedication and encouragement of two talented copyeditors, Candace Johnson, who enthusiastically supported the project, and Lee Robinson, who so clearly understood the power of Noémi's story. I will be forever grateful to my literary agent, Ivor Whitson, who tirelessly advocated for the book and believed in the power of Noémi's story. I also will never forget the support provided by Sarah Gillen, a good friend and author of *From Hurt to Joy*, who persisted in helping me with the challenging task of shortening the manuscript.

I would also like to acknowledge those who helped me at various points during my writing journey: Dr. Caroline Miller, a well-respected author who took the time to respond to an email from a stranger; William C. Dietz, a prolific author and friend, who patiently taught me about the realities of the unfamiliar world of nonacademic publishing; Chuck Robinson, author of *It Takes a Village Books: 35 Years of Building Community, One Book at a Time*, who generously shared his knowledge of the publishing world gained though his ownership of two local bookstores and leadership within

Acknowledgments

national book industry organizations; Joy Gilifen, president of our local Restorative Community Coalition, who clearly understood the importance of Noémi's story within the context of current societal issues; and Malcolm Stern, author of multiple books including *Slay Your Dragons with Compassion,* who read the manuscript and then introduced me to Eva Schloss, Holocaust survivor, stepsister of Anne Frank, and author of three books about the Holocaust, who also graciously reviewed the entire manuscript.

I also appreciate the time taken by a number of Noémi's former students in Missouri who thoughtfully shared their recollections of their time in Noémi's sixth-grade classroom and the impact she had on each of their lives. I also give thanks to Noémi's dear friends and Earnest's caregivers, Patty Roe and Harriette Wojciechowski, as well as to Noémi's granddaughters, Rachel Tefft, Julia Ban, and Miriam Ban, and Noémi's "adopted" granddaughter, Rumbidzayi Machiridza, for their encouragement and contributions. I will also be forever grateful for all of my behind-the-scenes cheerleaders, including my husband, David, and many special friends (you know who you are) who have read drafts, provided feedback, and who enthusiastically encouraged my efforts. I have tremendous gratitude for everyone who has helped make it possible for me to share Noémi's remarkable story.

Foreword

Thirty-six years ago, I was a high school teacher working with adolescents, many of whom were struggling with traumatic events in their lives. My son's pediatrician, Dr. Steven Ban, suggested I meet his mother, an award-winning elementary school teacher. In the years that followed, Noémi Ban and I became very close friends. From her, I learned a great deal about teaching my students and about dealing with life's challenges. I also learned about resilience as she described her own experiences and the loss of her family at Auschwitz-Birkenau. Eventually, Noémi (and two other survivors of pervasive trauma) became the focus of my Ph.D. research on trauma, literacy, and the pedagogy of hope.

Later, as a professor and director of a center for Holocaust, genocide, and ethnocide studies, I had the opportunity to work with many survivors of pervasive and prolonged trauma. Consistently they amazed me with their capacity to affirm the value of life in the face of death and to choose recovery in the face of humiliation and despair. Noémi took this a step further, effectively using stories from her own life to illustrate ways in which each of us can respond to our own challenges, losses, and disappointments. Noémi frequently spoke about the dangers of allowing hatred and bigotry to go unchecked, but she always did so with the greatest tenderness and love.

Noémi and I often discussed her recognition that many people today are dealing with abuse, bullying, violence, homophobia, bigotry, and hate, and are experiencing the same type of hurt as those who survived the Holocaust. She recognized the common experiences of being subjected to dehumanizing language, searching for someone to listen to our concerns, and sometimes encountering denial about terrible things that have happened. Noémi was more than a survivor. She was a profound source of wisdom and hope.

During the summer of 1995, Noémi asked me to accompany her as a friend and historiographer to what remains of the death camp at Auschwitz-Birkenau. For the first time since liberation, she stood on the ground where she had been imprisoned and where her dear ones were murdered. Deeply moved by her courage and strength, I documented as much as I could with photographs and copious notes. Upon our return, we put together a presentation to share with audiences at schools, universities, prisons, rehab centers, churches, and public libraries. Noémi went on to tell her story hundreds of times each year, over several decades. I was surprised by how restless students, recovering addicts, and people serving time in jail or prison, whose behaviors we might expect to be inattentive or disruptive, listened intently and asked meaningful questions (i.e., "Do you hate Germans?" "How can you have so much hope?" "How did you escape Hungary and come to America?" "Why did you decide to come to the United States?" "What was it like learning to read and write in English?" "What happened to your father?" "Are you concerned about the increasing hatred and bigotry that seem to be happening around the world?"). Noémi was frequently asked to address the question: "Doesn't it hurt to keep telling the painful parts of your story again and again? How can you keep doing it?" She would often respond, "Yes, it does hurt, but sharing is healing."

Noémi's story has been documented in many ways, for example

in her autobiographical children's book entitled *Sharing is Healing: A Holocaust Survivor's Story*, in a Western Washington University video "Lessons from the Holocaust: Confronting Hatred with Humanity," and in Jim Lortz's documentary *My Name is Noémi*. She was also interviewed and recorded by Steven Spielberg's Shoah Foundation. The primary focus in most of these works has been on Noémi's Holocaust testimony. However, while working on this book, Noémi was excited to expand beyond her Holocaust experiences to discuss the full story of her life. She wished to focus on the positive—a lifetime of events and relationships that made it possible for her to be a loving mother, grandmother, great-grandmother, teacher, and speaker. Describing the process of creating this book, Noémi explained to me, "This time I'm not being interviewed. I'm telling my good friend about what made me, 'me.' I'm telling her the whole story."

Dr. Diane Sue is eminently qualified to bring this "whole story" to life. Long before she and Noémi started this project, they shared decades of close friendship. Further, Diane's textbook writing has given her experience organizing and shaping large quantities of content for publication. Her academic and professional background gave her the training, skills, and patience to listen deeply, ask questions gently, and to conduct the supporting research required to authenticate and verify content. For example, she carefully read my dissertation and field notes from my travel to Auschwitz with Noémi, reviewed audio and video tapes of prior interviews, contacted historians, and spent time speaking with Noémi's former students and family members. Finally, Dr. Sue brought her vast experience in positive psychology to organize and present the content of her discussions with Noémi in ways which will enable the reader to gain a better understanding of how trauma can lead to compassion and healing. As you will see as you progress through the story, resiliency is possible even under the most catastrophic of circumstances.

During our 1995 visit to the remains at Auschwitz, I remember Noémi looking beyond the rusty barbed wire and into fields filled with wildflowers. She asked me, "Do you think that the ashes of my dear ones helped these flowers to grow?" At subsequent public events while sharing her story, I heard her express regret that her loved ones who died in the camp have no burial plot, no headstone. And then, she'd look directly into the eyes of those in attendance and say, "When I look and see the love in your eyes, I feel healing. Together we are creating a memorial."

Mrs. Noémi Ban, a beloved friend and family member, gifted speaker, synagogue elder, and survivor of unspeakable atrocity, passed away in 2019. Fortunately, Noémi's words, in her own voice, are preserved in the book you hold in your hands. Pull up a chair and enjoy.

Ray Wolpow
Professor Emeritus and former Director of the
Northwest Center for Holocaust, Genocide and Ethnocide
Education, Western Washington University

July 26, 2021

Introduction

Remarkable Resilience: The Life and Legacy of Noémi Ban Beyond the Holocaust is the story told to me by my dear friend, Noémi Schönberger Ban, a Hungarian American who survived imprisonment by the Nazis, sabotaged their bombs, faced Soviet oppression in Hungary, escaped into Austria, and then had a profound influence on thousands of people after she immigrated to the United States. Noémi's story not only underscores the true meaning of freedom and living life to the fullest but also illustrates our capacity to replace heartache and loss with love, hope, and faith in humankind. This book is a testament to Noémi's resilience and to the ways in which elders can make significant contributions to the lives of others.

I first met Noémi, a petite woman with silver-streaked black hair and a warm smile, in the early 1990s when my youngest daughter, then a middle school student, was working on an independent project about the Holocaust. Noémi had just begun to speak publicly about her experiences, and my daughter was the first student to interview her. Hearing her story is poignant under any circumstances, but it was particularly emotional for me because I was grieving the recent and sudden deaths of both my mother and grandmother. I listened to Noémi's story, told in her strong Hungarian accent, and could not hold back my tears. I felt immediate admiration and respect for someone who had endured incredible trauma yet spoke with such strength and with a spirit of hope.

After we first met, I sometimes had the pleasure of chatting with Noémi as she walked in our neighborhood on outings with her husband, a fellow Holocaust survivor, whose health was declining due to dementia and Parkinson's disease. Noémi's loving care for her husband touched my heart. Shortly after learning that her husband had passed, I invited Noémi to take a walk. Our discussions during that challenging time were the beginning of a deep and lasting friendship. Our relationship worked well because I tend to be a listener, whereas Noémi loved to talk and share whatever was on her mind. We were never short of conversation!

As the years passed and vigorous walks were no longer an option, we substituted shorter strolls, with Noémi using a cane for stability. Our outings eventually included Noémi's "Cadillac," as she called the bright red walker that replaced her cane. In later years, our visits took place in the kitchen or family room of Noémi's home, with much of our discussion focused on her past, particularly on the events that changed the course of her life. Nevertheless, her love of life and her gratitude for simple pleasures—including the freedom to take a sip of water if she was thirsty—never wavered.

I often wished someone would come forward to write a book about Noémi's remarkable life journey, including a focus on the depth and breadth of her contributions after the Holocaust. Several weeks before Noémi's ninety-sixth birthday, I suddenly realized that it made perfect sense for me to be the one to step up and help Noémi memorialize her story. When I proposed the idea to Noémi, she blew me a stream of kisses and replied, "This is the key! Our working together would be the best birthday present ever! At my honorable age, I know I won't live forever. You know me inside and out. You're the perfect person to write about my life! How soon can we begin?"

I understood I had an important job ahead of me. I also knew it would be a challenge. Wanting to make sure that anyone reading about Noémi would understand why she has been such an inspiration to so many people, I considered which of her characteristics were most important to capture. I wondered how I could adequately describe the courageous, spunky, determined, playful, and uplifting woman whom I was fortunate to call a dear friend.

One challenge that emerged almost immediately was the fact that Noémi's early life unfolded within a complex historical and socio-political context. So, as the book came together, I found it necessary to take a deep dive into European history. My writing was further aided by Noémi's translation of a tear-stained diary written by her father as he searched for his family in the final months of World War II and a subsequent memoir he wrote about his early life and some of his heartbreaking experiences before, during, and after the Holocaust.

The writing process itself was less challenging. Noémi and I worked together multiple days each week, and she was consistently organized, efficient, and motivated to address deep issues. I was careful to be punctual, aware that Noémi would be peering out her window patiently watching for me to appear, ready to maneuver her walker to the front door where she would warmly greet me and invariably announce, "I have a lot to tell you today!" On some occasions, as I arrived at the door, I was treated to the delightful sound of Noémi playing classical music on her beloved piano.

As with many things, Noémi had a strong opinion about how the writing process should work: "Diane, dear. Please, no machines! It will be you and me sitting down and talking, just as we always do. And if I'm jumping from this to that, we won't worry. I want people to realize that I'm not just a Holocaust survivor. There was a life before the Holocaust and a long life after the Holocaust, a life filled with love and happiness."

Many of our working hours involved our usual catch-up conversations, talking about whatever Noémi wanted to share, moving from topic to topic on the list clearly imprinted in her mind, often with laughter filling the room. Many times, Noémi repeated her favorite stories, usually prefaced with, "I know you have heard me say this before . . ." A common theme was her struggle to comprehend why people didn't stand up to the Nazis or to the Soviets. She was also distressed about the rise of authoritarianism occurring in countries around the world.

Noémi agreed that I could take notes, so as she chatted and answered my questions, I rapidly scribbled pages and pages of quotes, which I turned into manuscript drafts that I presented to Noémi for her comments or corrections. As Noémi reviewed each chapter, she underlined any words or sentences she wished to discuss in more detail. She was enthusiastic about what I was writing and frequently commented, "This is my life! This is exactly how it happened! I can hardly wait to read the whole book!"

Although we never spoke about it directly, Noémi and I both understood that I was writing for a time when Noémi was no longer with us. As I began the project, I found myself abruptly confronting the reality that someday there would be a world without Noémi's vibrant presence. I completed much of the writing in those first few weeks through the sheen of tears, acutely aware that in addition to honoring Noémi by sharing her story with a broader audience, I was preserving the memories of an extraordinary woman for whom I have tremendous love and respect.

This book brings Noémi's story to life for those who never had an opportunity to hear her speak, as well as provides additional insight into her life for those whose hearts she has already opened. The tens of thousands of people who have honored Noémi by listening to her story won't be surprised to learn that her resilience and strength spanned decades and allowed her to live a purpose-filled life well into her elder years. Even in her mid-nineties, Noémi joyously celebrated each day as a gift and as an opportunity to teach anyone who was willing to listen and learn. Noémi's goal with her public speaking was to create hope and to encourage people to embrace love and kindness—and to stand up to bigotry and hate. Now and in the future, we can honor Noémi by sharing her stories and her messages of courage, hope, and healing. There is no doubt that Noémi's wisdom will live on—just as her love lives on in every person she has touched.

Noémi always generously donated her time when speaking publicly, so she readily agreed to my suggestion that any author profits from this book go to charitable organizations focused on enhancing the lives of children or families, including those affected by present-day trauma and genocide. Details of organizations slated to receive any proceeds as well as more information about Noémi's parents and the historical background surrounding Noémi's story can be found on my website at **LivingWithResilience.com**.

Diane M. Sue
Bellingham, Washington

Part I

Europe
1922–1944

1

My Delight

1922–1932

The story of my life begins with a tale of love that evolved into a never-ending bond between my parents, Samu and Juliska—a partnership strengthened by years of mutual affection and respect. Their relationship developed slowly, deepened rapidly, and ended tragically. Because of their love and devotion, my early years were filled with security and family unity. I learned how to be strong from watching my parents and their commitment to family and to each other. Those memories have given me both courage and resilience during difficult times.

In the early years of World War I, just before his twentieth birthday and weeks after he met my mom, my father was drafted to serve in the Austro-Hungarian military and was deployed to the Russian front. He soon was taken captive by the Russian army and imprisoned in Siberia. Even after Russia withdrew from World War I, my father's imprisonment dragged on, and the months of constant hunger, forced labor, and severe weather turned into years. It was six years before my father was finally able to return to Hungary and reconnect with my mom. Although they had met only once prior to the war, my parents exchanged letters throughout my father's years of imprisonment, and my father asked for my mom's hand in marriage the first time he saw her after he returned home.

I was born in Szeged, Hungary, on September 29, 1922, exactly nine months after my parents married. My mother chose my name, Noémi, which means "my delight." My early years were a beautiful time of my life. My mother and I were always very close, the best of friends. We trusted each other and talked about anything and everything. My mom openly shared her thoughts with me, and that's how I learned. Those priceless conversations helped me appreciate the world around me and allowed me to grow as a person.

I also learned a great deal by watching my parents. Their marriage was really something! They supported each other and had a strong connection. My dad had a high opinion of my mom, so he shared everything with her and valued her judgment. They were true partners. Together they helped me to learn to think independently and to face challenges without backing down. In those idyllic years, I don't think they ever imagined the challenges that they were preparing me to face.

2

Impossible to Escape History

1928–1943

Both my mom and my dad wanted me to have the opportunity to play a musical instrument, so they saved their money, and when I was five or six years old, they bought a glossy, black grand piano. They arranged for me to take weekly lessons, the beginning of many joyful hours of surrounding myself with music. My mom enjoyed listening to my daily practice, always smiling at my delight as I played my favorite songs. I'll never forget the tears of joy that filled her eyes whenever my father sat beside me, accompanying me on his violin.

When I was nine years old, my little sister, Erzsébet, was born, and we moved into a cozy, two-bedroom house close to the school where my father was a teacher and the school principal. I was excited not only to have a younger sister, but also to experience the luxury of indoor plumbing! Erzsébet and I became very close and were quite a pair. I had our mom's petite stature, dark eyes, and wavy, jet-black

4

hair, while Erzsébet was tall and slender with curly, brown hair like our father. Erzsébet's glasses made her look quite serious, but she had a fantastic sense of humor. She always kept a straight face when telling jokes and enjoyed making everyone laugh. Erzsébet learned quickly and had wisdom beyond her years.

Since I was almost ten years older than Erzsébet, I was very much the big sister and someone whom Erzsébet relied on. Erzsébet seemed to think that a big sister knows everything. She constantly asked for my advice, and often mentioned, "I want to be just like you, Noémi." Although we had a wonderful relationship, I must admit that we weren't angels. We sometimes argued. That can happen when a big sister speaks frankly to a little sister and the little sister doesn't like what the big sister is saying. But we loved and respected each other, and that's what was most important.

My grandma Nina, a petite woman with a kind face and an easy smile, was a big part of my early years. She had a gorgeous singing voice. I remember her belting out her favorite songs while she tended the carefully organized rows of vegetables and flowers she planted in our yard. Grandma Nina enjoyed baking and always had delicious smells coming from her kitchen. I smile when I think of the wonderful food my grandma prepared, especially the special treats always awaiting me when I came to visit.

Every Friday night our family's celebration of the Sabbath was the highlight of the week. Our house was filled with the aroma of freshly baked challah (traditional Jewish bread) and the anticipation of being together. My grandma Nina often joined us. She or my mom would light the Shabbat candles, and my father would bless the bread and wine as we began our meal. After eating, we sat together in the living room, quietly reading and enjoying each other's company. Friday evenings were always slow, quiet, and peaceful. Something extraordinary and beautiful—a silent trust and shared affection—surrounded us and filled us with serenity. I felt so protected and loved in those special hours each week—an inner sense of peace and harmony that has remained with me.

My father wanted our family to have a strong Hungarian identity in addition to our Jewish traditions, so it's not surprising that I grew up feeling proud to be both Jewish and Hungarian. I loved Hungarian music, art, and literature and felt a strong bond with Hungarian cultural life. In this respect, I felt no different from my Christian friends.

Soon after I graduated from high school, during a visit to Szeged to see a family friend, I met Ernő, a high school mathematics teacher whom my father knew through the Jewish teachers' group. Ernő seemed interested in me, and my parents thought we would make a good match. I didn't agree. I told them that Ernő was much too old for me. I was eighteen, and he was the ripe old age of twenty-eight. I spoke so strongly that my parents got the message and didn't mention him again.

Around this same time, Adolph Hitler and his Nazi movement had become quite powerful. It became impossible to ignore what we were hearing about anti-Semitic violence and restrictive Jewish laws spreading across Europe. Although my parents worked hard to protect Erzsébet and me from these concerns and from the prejudice directed at those of us who were Jewish, I overheard family discussions about things such as the ridiculous "blood libel" stories claiming that Jews supposedly kidnapped and murdered Christian children to use their blood to make matzo, the unleavened bread we prepare during Passover. Although there was no truth to these stories, some people

believed and repeated these lies. I also heard that some people accepted the nonsense that Hitler and other fascists kept repeating—claims
of Jewish conspiracies and accusations that the Jewish people were
responsible for the German and Hungarian losses in World War I.
Sadly, it didn't take long for these repeated lies to become accepted as
if they were true.

Some of our family members (and many other Jews) began to
discover that the increasing anti-Semitism was affecting their ability
to earn a living. Our relatives who owned a small grocery store in
Hungary's capital city, Budapest, told my parents about the owner of
a competing store who was regularly standing outside his own store,
pointing to their business and yelling, "Don't go to that store! They
are dirty Jews! We sell the very same goods, so you don't even need
to go close to them. Stay away!" My parents paid close attention and
became increasingly worried about what Jewish families might face
next.

Although I had received my acceptance into the local teachers'
training program, my mother suggested that I postpone college. I
was very disappointed to miss the opportunity to become a teacher—something I had dreamed of since I was young. However, my
parents both agreed it was better for me to learn a skill I could use to
maintain myself or help the family in case the situation with Hitler
became worse. Not long afterward, I was grateful for their idea of
having me learn a practical skill—a plan that may have helped save
my life.

Instead of beginning college, I left our family home in Kiskunhalas
and moved to Budapest, where I lived with my father's sister, my aunt
Lina, a recent widow who had two young sons. My parents had been
concerned about Aunt Lina since the death of her husband and were
happy that I could help her and keep her company. I was offered a

job as a seamstress at a fancy shop owned by a family friend. My mom had taught me to mend and to do needlework, so I had a bit of experience sewing before I started—but I had a lot to learn. The store sold all kinds of clothing and goods—lingerie, swimsuits, dresses, fancy linen—to the rich people who shopped at the store, like the wife of the famous Hungarian composer Béla Bartók. Their customers even included Magda, Eva, and Zsa Zsa Gábor, the famous Gábor sisters who later moved to America. Although I wasn't happy to be in Budapest, I have a pretty flexible personality. If I have no way out of a situation, I do my best to make the situation as comfortable as possible. Slowly, I got into the mood of learning more about sewing, and it turned out all right. It was like a regular job, and riding the streetcar every day was somewhat of an adventure since it was my first experience living in a large city.

I had some wonderful opportunities during the time I was in Budapest. I had always been very close to my father's brother, Uncle Simon, and his wife, Aunt Berta. They never had children and treated me like their own. Uncle Simon taught literature and history in a local public high school and Aunt Berta, a native of Austria and a talented musician, gave piano lessons. Aunt Berta, always happy to speak her native German, helped me become even more fluent in the language. I was lucky to have that extra assistance because speaking and understanding German became extremely important during some especially challenging times ahead of me.

Uncle Simon and Aunt Berta both loved music, so we often went to concerts or to the theater. Aunt Berta's brother, Otto Rauch, was a well-known Austrian journalist and a very nice man. Because of his work, he often received a pair of front-row tickets to the Budapest opera, allowing me an opportunity to attend with him or with Uncle Simon or Aunt Berta. I even attended concerts alone when no one was available to accompany me. What a special time that was! I didn't even know you usually had to pay for tickets because it was always taken care of. I had no idea how lucky I was.

Soon after I began working in Budapest, my parents moved to Debrecen, a city in the northeastern part of Hungary. My father loved his job in the tiny city of Kiskunhalas, but the enrollment of Christian students in his school was declining—apparently in response to the anti-Semitic propaganda that had spread from Nazi Germany to Hungary. Needing to find a more secure job, he accepted a new position as the principal of a Jewish elementary school in Debrecen. Soon after, my uncle Simon, who had taught in a non-Jewish school for years, was fired from his position—just because he was Jewish.

As the war came closer, my parents became increasingly worried about what they were hearing and suggested that I come live with them in Debrecen. Just like the decision to postpone college when my parents were concerned about the spread of Nazism, I listened to their concerns. In those days, if your parents suggested something, you didn't argue—you just did it. I also believed in their good judgment. Additionally, I was well aware of the war surrounding us and recognized that it was getting much closer to Hungary. I understood that the situation was serious and that it was important to return home. Within days, my father arrived on the train to escort me back to Debrecen, and I bid a tearful farewell to Aunt Lina and my two young cousins, unaware that I would never see them again. I had no idea just how quickly our lives would change.

3

The Threat Comes Closer

1943–1944

As concern about the Nazis filled the air, my mother discovered that she was pregnant. The year of her pregnancy, 1943, was a very difficult year. We knew the situation was growing worse in Germany and in Poland, and we had no idea what Hitler would do next. We had an uneasy feeling but very little information. Most people were staying close to home, so we were surprised when Ernő, the man I had met in Szeged, decided to stop by on his way to visit his sisters. This time, my mom didn't suggest that I should show more interest in him. My parents' main concerns were my mom's pregnancy and the war surrounding Hungary. We all knew that my mom's age increased the risk of birth complications, so my father and I watched her carefully, not wanting the pregnancy to endanger her life. Neither of us wanted to risk losing her.

My dear mother was forty-three years old when, on December 30, 1943, my baby brother, Gábor, was born after a very difficult labor and delivery. The traumatic birth didn't keep us from celebrating the arrival of a healthy baby boy. Unfortunately, the months following Gábor's birth were as challenging as the night he was born. My mother was delighted to have a son, but she was very ill. She had developed thrombosis involving a blood clot in her leg which left the entire limb badly swollen and very painful. The doctor told my mom to stay in bed and move as little as possible because the clot could kill her if it shifted to her heart, lungs, or brain.

During the months that my mother remained in bed, I helped as much as I could. Those days weren't easy—taking care of my mom, my sister, and the baby and looking out for my grandmother. I was relieved that my father was there to help once he returned from work each evening. I recall how frightened Erzsébet was during that time; she often held tightly to my hand or followed closely behind me as I moved quickly through the house, trying to keep up with all the work. It was also challenging because Erzsébet, accustomed to being the youngest child, was a bit jealous of Gábor. She was no longer the baby of the family and missed our undivided attention.

The day my mother was finally well enough to leave her bed was a memorable day. Gábor was almost three months old. We thought we would be celebrating the improvement in my mother's health—and the opportunity for her to begin to walk again and regain her strength, enjoying the outdoors as our long winter ended and hints of spring filled the air. But that's not what happened.

Unfortunately, the day my mom finally stepped out of bed was the very same day the Nazi troops began their occupation of Hungary. Hungarian leaders had managed to keep the Nazis out of the country to that point, but suddenly their strategy failed. And when Hitler's troops moved in, the Hungarian Nazis—members of an anti-Semitic group called the Arrow Cross—were ready and waiting, eager to help the German Nazis with their plans to destroy the Jews and other groups they hated. The Hungarian Nazis celebrated the fact that their time had finally come—and they weren't the least bit hesitant to wield their power. It was a terrifying day for all of us. I will never forget the look of panic on my mother's face as she stood staring out of her bedroom window, astonished to see armed Nazis marching through the streets and horrified by the realization that war had arrived at our doorstep.

Part II

1944–1945

4

No Longer a Friendly Place

March–April 1944

Hitler's Nazi troops swept in and began their occupation of Hungary on March 19, 1944. Soon, the Hungarian Nazis—the Arrow Cross—and local police officers were knocking on the doors of everyone known to be Jewish. Anyone with more than one Jewish grandparent was considered Jewish, including Hungarians who had converted to Christianity or who had never practiced Judaism. According to the new laws, we were allowed to leave our home only during certain hours and we were required to wear a yellow cloth badge cut in the shape of the Star of David and marked with the word *Jude*, a signal to everyone that we were Jewish.

It took little effort for the Nazis to magnify and ignite the underlying prejudice that had been simmering for years. It all happened with such ease—hateful words inflamed the anti-Semitic leanings of many Hungarians, and our lives were forever changed. They forced us to wear the badges so they could more easily control and stigmatize us. Within a matter of days, people casually accepted the vilification of Jewish men, women, and children. We felt like trash, easily cast aside and forgotten. The first time I stepped out wearing the yellow star, I wanted to run home and hide. That mark of hate was there for the whole world to see—people who were sympathetic as well as those who looked at us with disdain. We were suddenly different—inferior. Sadly, many Hungarians seemed to welcome the Nazis' efforts against us.

My parents began speaking to me more openly about anti-Semitism and the Nazis. I spoke to my mother about a book I had read—Franz Werfel's *The Forty Days of Musa Dagh*—about the Turkish government's use of concentration camps and genocide against Armenians during World War I. At the time I read the book, I had no idea we would find ourselves in a similar situation, with the Nazis targeting the Jews just as the Turks had come for the Armenians. I told my mom that it felt like the same thing was happening to us, thirty years later. My mom agreed it was impossible to ignore the similarities.

The occupying Nazis soon created a Jewish ghetto and ordered all Jews to remain in that region of the city. Armed soldiers and local police officers guarded the ghetto perimeter day and night. We were not allowed to leave nor speak with anyone on the outside. Seeing their guns and not knowing what would happen if we disobeyed, we followed their orders. We became prisoners in the ghetto. We had no choice.

Our house happened to be located within the ghetto, so unlike Jewish families living outside the boundaries, we remained in our home. However, the Nazi commanders assigned eight families to live with us—filling our small house with strangers displaced from their own homes, each bringing only a small amount of food and a change of clothing. There was not nearly enough space for everyone. Even with one or two families squeezed into each room, some people had to sleep in the hallway. We had only one kitchen, of course, so everyone took turns cooking. Although we had one full bathroom and another with a toilet and a sink, there was always a line of people awaiting their turn. The living circumstances were especially difficult for the elders, like my grandmother, who were accustomed to their privacy and their routines.

Although the rules allowed shopping within the ghetto during certain hours, the store shelves were often empty, and we soon ran out of food. My mother shared some potatoes stored in our basement, but there wasn't enough for everyone. As food became scarce, my mom, and the other mothers who were breastfeeding, had difficulty producing milk.

Each Friday evening, we continued to celebrate the Sabbath, taking care not to run out of candles. One Friday, someone managed to find the ingredients to bake a loaf of traditional bread for the Sabbath meal; the aroma of freshly baked challah evoked memories of life before the Nazis and temporarily lifted our spirits. On another occasion, the women made a pot of chicken and vegetable soup for everyone to share, another shiny moment during those difficult days.

Throughout my growing-up years and as a young adult, I treasured the grand piano that my parents had purchased when I was just beginning school. A few weeks after the Nazis created the ghetto, a group of workmen knocked loudly on our door and entered the house without waiting to be invited. One of the men announced, without apology, that they had come to take away our piano. I was heartbroken watching them carry away my beloved piano and was unable to hold back my tears. It's hard to explain just how hard it was to lose that piano. It felt like someone had died and the men had come to carry away the body.

Fear was our constant companion during those days in the ghetto. We were facing a double threat—the unknown danger from the Nazis and from the war itself. We frequently heard air raid sirens because the Soviets, joining the Allies in their fight against the Hungarians and Germans, were dropping bombs over Debrecen. The warning sirens, sounding both day and night, prompted everyone to rush down to our basement, which was nothing more than a small, unfinished storage area. There we waited, huddled together. Even when the "all clear" siren sounded, we were well aware that we were still not safe.

My father—considered one of the leaders of the Jewish community because he was a school principal—worked with the local Jewish Council, who assigned him the task of leaving the ghetto early each day to meet with the Nazi commander. My father was told to appear at the Gestapo building and wait for the Nazi leader at seven o'clock each morning. Although he arrived on time as ordered, my father often waited two or three hours until the commander finally called him with a short whistle and a beckoning finger—like someone might call a dog. The commander expected my father to immediately run down the long corridor, and took pleasure in sending him back multiple times if he didn't run fast enough. The cruel commander sometimes forced my father to run down the corridor on all fours while he and his colleagues stood by laughing. One morning my father fell asleep while waiting on the bench. He was rudely awakened when a whip hit his head and the commander shouted, "Lazy pig! Impudent Jew! You're strictly forbidden to sit here and dirty the bench. March! Get out! Scram!" Not wanting my mother to learn how disgracefully the Nazis were treating him, my father never spoke to us or anyone else about these indignities. Instead, day after day, he silently carried the burden of this dehumanizing treatment; I only learned about these events decades later when reading my father's journal.

From the minute the Nazis invaded Hungary, we realized that something horrible was occurring; however, we had no idea what was coming next. That was the Nazis' way—to keep us fearful and uncertain. That strategy decreased our resistance; we believed it in our best interest to cooperate rather than make trouble. Uncertainty also gave us room for hope because we had no idea that things would get worse. How could we possibly imagine what was coming? This was part of the Nazis' success. We didn't know what was happening until the very second that it occurred.

5

Carrying On

May–June 1944

Our situation in the ghetto grew more dire on May 23, 1944, when orders arrived commanding every Jewish man between the ages of eighteen and fifty-five to report for work service early the next morning. Work service was the Nazis' name for forced labor—prisoners working without pay. Slave laborers were required to go wherever the Nazis took them and to do whatever the Nazis told them to do. The men dug ditches, built railways, carried supplies, worked in factories, or helped the brutal Nazi soldiers.

My dear father, who was forty-eight years old, realized he had no choice but to follow their demands. I remember how my mom stayed close to his side as he packed his knapsack. My parents didn't sleep at all that night. They recognized that the troubling times they had hoped would never materialize were upon us and that we were all in danger. They planned where they would meet if they survived the war—if they were able to flee Hungary, they would meet in Tel Aviv

19

or New York. My mother couldn't stop crying, and my father gently held her in his arms, quietly wiping away the tears trickling down his own cheeks.

Just before leaving the house, my father said a blessing for my mother, my sister, and me. He then put his hands on my baby brother's head and said a special prayer. When my father turned to bless my grandmother, she blessed him first, her eyes brimming with tears as she wished him well. Trying not to alarm my sister, my father casually kissed her goodbye as if he expected to return. Then he silently walked out the door. I will never forget that day or the days that followed. I never again saw my mother smile. Instead, sadness and heartbreak were permanently etched on her face.

When the Nazis took my father away, I had no choice but to be strong. My father had done whatever he could to make our life in the ghetto bearable, but he was gone. Although I was only twenty-one, I became the head of the family. All of us who remained in the ghetto—the mothers, the grandmothers and grandfathers, the young children, and young women like me—faced constant fear.

The soldiers brought more women and children into our house to take the place of the men forced to leave. Although surrounded by people, my mother and I felt completely alone. She constantly spoke about my father, convinced that she would never see him again. She was still recovering from her illness, so I continued helping care for Gábor, who was not yet six months old. I fed him formula and changed his diapers, often with Erzsébet holding my hand or following close behind me. It was also a challenging time for Erzsébet—almost a teenager but still very much a child—who had constant questions and voiced many of the same anxieties constantly circling through my mind: "Where is our father?" "When is he coming back?" "What will happen to us?" "Will this ever end?" I had no answers for her. After my father left, we had no word from him or the others—none at all. And we had absolutely no idea what might happen next.

During this time, I had an opportunity to escape. Several teenaged boys, who remained in the ghetto because they were too young for forced labor, were working with an underground resistance group, using a hidden printing machine to create false identification papers. One of these young men encouraged me to leave, offering to create papers that would give me a new name—a Christian identity so I could hide from the Nazis by posing as a Christian maid and working for people willing to help hide Jews. I had a sense of foreboding that I just couldn't shake—a feeling that something terrible was going to happen and that I needed to stay—so I told the persistent teenager that I appreciated his offer, but that I could not and would not leave my family. I didn't tell my mother about the offer. I made my decision quickly, and I didn't look back.

Our house was on the very edge of the ghetto, overlooking a road in the free world where people still walked the streets and vehicles still traveled. At first, we were able to peek out of the windows and watch people who were continuing with their lives as if nothing of concern had happened—knowing we were there yet appearing completely oblivious to the human beings imprisoned in the ghetto. One day some workmen came to our house carrying large boards. The men nailed the boards across every window on the street-side of our house. Once the windows were covered, the feeling of being a prisoner was so intense that a woman living with us started to sob, crying out, "I feel like I'm in my own coffin with those men nailing the lid closed on me!" I knew exactly how she was feeling.

Fortunately, the men forgot to cover the glass opening in our storage attic. So every single day, Erzsébet and I climbed the ladder to the attic and peeked out the window, saying hello to freedom and making a wish that we would soon be released. We hadn't lost hope that our father would come back and that our lives would return to normal. Watching people outside the ghetto helped us believe the world we had once known might magically reappear.

6

The Outside World Turns Away

June 1944

The Hungarian Nazis delighted in delivering each new order that further reduced our freedom. We had been in the ghetto for almost three months when they told us that we would be leaving early the next morning. They said we could each carry one package containing a small pillow, a bed sheet, a small amount of dry food, and one change of underwear. They warned us not to bring anything else. We were all growing weaker from lack of food and constant stress, so there was some relief in knowing we would be leaving the ghetto. Yet, we still had no idea where the Nazis planned to take us. We also wondered how the men would locate us when they returned, but we were too frightened to ask. We realized we had no choice except to obey the order. Every step of the way we had complied—doing what we were told to do and becoming what they wanted us to be. Once again, we were obedient. No questions and no answers.

Early the next morning, we dutifully stood outside in the yard, each holding one small package—just as we had been ordered to do. With so much uncertainty surrounding us, few of us had slept during the night, so we were exhausted even before the guards ordered us to march toward the gates of the ghetto. Before we left the ghetto boundaries, we faced one more indignity. To ensure we had no hidden valuables, Arrow Cross soldiers randomly searched people, taking those selected one at a time into a house near the ghetto entrance. When the guards ordered me to undergo a search, my mother refused to permit me to be alone with the soldiers. Having been warned that the searches were quite intimate, she adamantly refused to leave my side, continuously repeating, "I'm going in with her!" until the guards finally acquiesced. The Arrow Cross men examined me everywhere, carefully feeling my body, including all crevices, to see if I had anything hidden. It was incredibly shocking and humiliating to be touched in that way. Although I was embarrassed for my mother to see what they were doing, I was grateful to have her with me. The guards then pushed us toward the crowd of people waiting by the ghetto gates.

Eventually, the guards ordered all of us to leave the ghetto, forcing us to march through the streets of Debrecen wearing our yellow stars. Along with others with limited mobility, guards put my grandmother, baby brother, and mother in a horse-drawn wagon. Erzsébet and I walked together, along with thousands of other silent ghetto residents. For the first time in weeks, we were outside the locked gates of the ghetto; yet, we were still not free. The Hungarian Nazis guarded us every step of the way.

Non-Jewish residents lined the streets, watching us as we solemnly left the ghetto, each holding our small package. I reached out to comfort Erzsébet, who was clinging tightly to my hand and trembling as she tried to keep up with the surging crowd moving along the street. I did my best to hold my head up high—trying not to show my fear and embarrassment—as we were pushed forward within the mass of Jewish prisoners. As we stumbled along confused and terrified, I could see that some people watching us were holding handkerchiefs and wiping away tears. However, many more were loudly applauding, rejoicing as we were forced from the city for no reason other than the "crime" of having Jewish blood.

7

Waiting and Still Hoping

June 1944

After walking for miles, we reached a large, poorly maintained building where hundreds of people were already waiting. As soon as we arrived, Arrow Cross guards used their guns and bayonets to force us inside the building—a barren, deserted place previously used for making and storing bricks. Everywhere I looked, I saw terrified people; some were standing, but many, malnourished and exhausted from the walk, were sitting or lying on the floor. I looked for my mother and grandmother but couldn't find them. A guard, who had ordered us to climb the ladder leading to the second floor, became impatient and jabbed me with his bayonet when I stopped to take one last look for my mother.

Once upstairs, Erzsébet and I frantically looked for our loved ones. Unable to locate them in the crowded attic, I became convinced that the Nazis had taken them somewhere else. Erzsébet and I finally stopped searching and collapsed onto the dirty floor, crying inconsolably. A neighbor approached, saying, "I saw your family over in the corner of the attic." I was flooded with relief when I spotted my mom holding Gábor tightly to her chest as my grandma tried to soothe him by rubbing his back. We all embraced, crying and laughing at the same time. Erzsébet and I once again felt safe, certain that being together somehow protected us. After those terrifying hours, nothing was more important than remaining together.

We waited in that factory for days—crowded together in the dirt-covered attic. We were relieved to have our sheets and pillows to sit on, but we suffered from the summer heat during the day and from the lack of blankets during the night. We had been malnourished before we arrived and still had little access to food or water. Each day our hunger and thirst increased, and so did our fear. Erzsébet became increasingly thin and was constantly hungry. My mother cried each time Erzsébet asked for food and there was nothing to give her. If we wanted to get a sip of water or use the filthy toilet, we needed to climb up and down the ladder, not an easy task for my mom and grandmother. My little brother, who was six months old, needed formula and clean diapers, so tending to his needs kept me busy. I used water from a well in the brickyard to rinse out his diapers each morning and did my best to warm his formula, placing his bottle in a pile of sun-heated bricks.

What we were going through was hard enough for healthy people, but my mother suffered tremendously in the extremely crowded conditions. She was still recovering from her illness and wore bandages on her swollen leg. One morning when she was returning to the attic after using the bathroom, I saw a teenaged guard hit her with a whip. It broke my heart to see her treated that way, but there was nothing I could do to protect her.

We spent hours sitting and waiting, not knowing what we were waiting for. Then one morning the guards began calling people by name and occupational group. As people disappeared, we began to wonder where the Nazis were taking them. We heard a rumor that families of teachers, lawyers, and doctors would be going to Austria. We also heard that those of us in the attic would be going to a place called Auschwitz, but we had no idea where that was.

All of a sudden, the guards called our names, ordering us to take our packages and immediately line up downstairs. When we finally exited the building, I hoped that wherever we were going next would be a better place. Perhaps we would return to our crowded house in the ghetto, or if they sent us to Austria, perhaps the Austrians would welcome us. Certainly, anywhere we went would be an improvement over the living conditions in that brick factory. At that point, I still had hope.

8

Packed

Late June 1944

The Arrow Cross soldiers led our group to the railroad yard next to the brick factory. Waiting there were uniformed German Nazis, members of the elite Schutzstaffel (SS), beside a long line of enclosed, wooden cattle cars. The SS guards began yelling at us in German as they pushed us forward, freely using their bayonets if someone was not moving fast enough. Other SS soldiers pushed us into a cattle car—loudly counting each person—then ordered us to sit down. Although it was impossible for everyone to find a place to sit, the SS soldiers continued yelling for everyone to get on the floor. We did our best to obey, but some of us had no choice but to awkwardly sit on total strangers. I helped my mother settle in with Gábor in her lap, and then made sure my grandmother and Erzsébet found a place to sit beside them. I found a place between them. Erzsébet tightly grasped my hand, refusing to let go.

I noticed two empty buckets and, wondering about their purpose,

29

I decided to use my knowledge of German to ask one of the guards. I now realize it was dangerous to ask questions, but at that time, we had little direct experience with German soldiers. I wanted to understand what was going on. I wanted to know. The guard pointed to one bucket and said it was for "sanitary purposes." He was telling us that the bucket was what eighty-five people would use as a toilet! He also said that the other container would hold drinking water for us to share. I cannot even begin to describe the dread we felt as the guards stepped out of the cattle car and closed the doors, leaving us trapped inside. The unforgettable sound of the latch closing signaled the final step in the Nazis' theft of our freedom. We soon heard the haunting sound of a train whistle as the cattle car slowly began to move.

The only air and light came from the cracks between the boards and two small windows covered with barbed wire. With tiny babies, young children, teenagers, older men, and women of all ages packed together, the cattle car was incredibly hot as we traveled day after day. And each time the train stopped, the stifling conditions grew worse. We were sure we would suffocate. With the oppressive summer heat and humidity, combined with our lack of food, water, and sleep, it wasn't long before our thinking became foggy. Our thirst was overwhelming, especially because the guards only refilled the water once.

Although we were embarrassed to use the small bucket as a toilet, we had no other choice. At first, everyone made an effort to maintain privacy by holding up a sheet, but we were soon too exhausted and bewildered to care about modesty. The guards never once emptied the bucket. However, after spending so many days in the sweltering brickyard, we were malnourished and dehydrated, so it took a while for the bucket to overflow with human waste and spill onto the floor. It was summer, and a nauseating smell permeated the air of our wooden prison. The lack of fresh air, the heat, and the stench were unbearable.

I still had a small package with items for my baby brother, although all that remained was a sugar cube and a tiny bit of formula. Little Gábor was crying constantly. He screamed when he had no food, but also when we tried to feed him. Once when we stopped, someone handed in a bucket of water. Little Gábor had fainted, so I asked the SS soldier if I could get him some water, and he gave me permission to fill Gábor's bottle. However, when I turned back toward my family, the guard used his rifle to knock the bottle out of my hand, spilling the water onto the people around me. The treatment we were receiving from the German SS guards terrified all of us, young and old alike. I smelled the odor of pure fear in our stifling prison. Many were shocked into silence, while others screamed in terror.

The conditions in the cattle car were especially difficult for my grandmother, and, like many of us, she became increasingly withdrawn. One day she suddenly woke from her lethargy, stood up, and began shouting, "It's not yours! It's mine! Nobody can take it away from me!" I didn't understand what she was talking about, but I could see she was terribly upset. I reached out, trying to calm her by reassuring her that no one was taking anything from her. It was then that she reached down and pulled a tall, silver candleholder from under her long skirt. She continued shouting, "This is mine! I have it! Nobody can take it away from me!" In that moment, I not only understood what she meant but also realized that she was in serious trouble. As my grandmother held up the candleholder, a cold fear settled over the cattle car. Around us, there was total silence. We all recognized the peril. The Arrow Cross had told us many times to leave all of our valuables behind and she had not followed the rules. If the Nazis discovered my grandmother had disobeyed, I feared they might kill her.

Frozen with terror, I knew I had to do something and do it quickly. My grandma was quite confused, and I had no idea what she might do next. Deciding that I needed to take the candleholder away from her, I hugged her, attempting to soothe her as I slowly pried her fingers from the precious keepsake and then quickly tucked it away. My grandma was quietly sobbing, and I felt her fragile body shaking beneath my embrace before she collapsed onto the floor. My grandmother's mind seemed far away, and she made no further mention of the beloved family heirloom—apparently forgetting that I had pried it from her fingers and hid it deep within the pile of packages on the floor of the cattle car.

I was grateful when the train finally stopped and the SS guards opened the doors. I took a deep breath, feeling incredible relief as fresh air seeped into the cattle car. Each time we were given a reprieve from our misery, however, we soon learned that the Nazis had something more horrendous in store for us. That was their philosophy. They made the suffering—the appalling circumstances they created—so terrible that we eventually got to a point where we didn't care what was happening; we just wanted it to end. We had been relieved to leave the ghetto, and then the brick factory, and now the cattle car. We continued to believe that it could not possibly get worse. Unfortunately, we were once more tragically mistaken. We had arrived at Auschwitz II-Birkenau, a Nazi camp built with a single purpose—to destroy as many prisoners as possible. We learned much later that we were among the last prisoners transported to Auschwitz. We arrived on July 1, 1944. The final group arrived ten days later.

9

No Time for Tears

Early July 1944

A t Auschwitz II-Birkenau, the SS officers who surrounded us were even more cruel than the SS guards who had forced us onto the train in Debrecen. As the soldiers yelled orders, men dressed in striped outfits, apparently prisoners, began urging us to move forward. Worried about my brother, I asked one of the helpers if I could bring Gábor's remaining formula with us, pleading in German, "What will happen to the baby if he has no food?" The prisoner replied, "You can't bring anything with you. You won't need it." The prisoner then asked how many people were in my family. When I told him there were five of us, he responded with a simple statement, "I'm sorry." I didn't understand what he meant, or why his face was filled with such sadness.

On the train platform, growling dogs and SS soldiers carrying guns and bayonets surrounded us. The guards pushed the elderly men and boys to one side and yelled for the women and girls to line up in pairs. After being in cramped quarters for days, it was not easy to walk. I stood beside my mother, who was carrying Gábor in her arms. Erzsébet and my grandmother lined up behind us. By that time, my grandmother was so weak that she could barely stand, and she seemed to be in a complete daze.

Standing on a small platform at the front of the line was an SS officer wearing white gloves, well-shined shoes, and a fancy white uniform. We were standing in front of someone who, with one swift movement, would change the course of our lives. At that time, I didn't know that the man was Josef Mengele. He looked briefly at whoever was standing in front of him and then motioned to his right or left with his horsewhip. Everyone obediently moved in the direction that Mengele pointed—to the right or to the left. I noticed that older people, young children, and babies with their mothers were going one way, whereas younger women were sent the other way. As we neared the front of the line, my mother put Gábor under her jacket in an effort to hide and protect him. Dazed and exhausted, my grandmother slowly shuffled forward but seemed unaware of what was occurring. Erzsébet looked terrified and kept reaching for my hand.

Finally, my mother and I were at the front of the line. Showing no emotion, Mengele raised his whip and made a quick movement, signaling for my mother and Gábor and then my grandmother and Erzsébet to move to the left. After looking briefly at me, he signaled to the right. In that instant, with no time for goodbyes, I was separated from the rest of my family. I looked at my mother in alarm, and she gave me a long, sad look. I could see she was worried that I was going to be all alone. Neither of us understood what was happening, but her beautiful eyes seemed to be communicating, "Noémi, I love you. Take care." The guards were already starting to yell at me to move. My heart was breaking, but there was no time for tears. I had no choice but to go.

The Nazis were successful in planning a system where we had no room for anger or rebellion. Large German shepherds barked at us and nipped at our heels as the SS soldiers pushed us into a large room where more prisoners were helping the Nazis write down our names. Still clinging to hope, I thought, *If they are asking for details about us and having us sign a paper, they won't do anything drastic with us.* I learned years later that the Nazis were recording our names because they wanted to be very precise about the location of each of their prisoners.

What happened next was beyond human imagination. SS guards ordered us to undress and to carry our shoes, cautioning us to remember where we put our clothes so we could retrieve them. We followed their orders, realizing we had no choice. We passed a room with human hair piled from floor to ceiling, neatly sorted and organized by color. My body shook uncontrollably as a prisoner hurriedly cut my hair and shaved my head, and then came the indignity of someone shaving the private parts of my body. All around me, I saw terrified women without hair and without clothing. It was almost impossible to distinguish one of us from the other—the Nazis not only wanted to take away our pride but also our identity.

The SS guards crowded us into another large room with showerheads high on the ceiling. We stood shivering with fear as we waited for someone to turn on the shower. My shaking intensified when icy water began pouring out of the showerheads above us. When the spray abruptly stopped, we once again waited, crowded together and completely drenched, without any clothes or towels to cover us. We held on to our shoes, now soaking wet. The guards ordered us to form a line and begin marching, yelling for us to catch one of the tattered dresses they were throwing into the air. We each put on the garment we caught even if it didn't fit. We had no underwear and no sanitary products for those of us who were menstruating. That was our welcome to Auschwitz II-Birkenau.

Tricking us was part of the Nazi secret—we never knew if we were hearing the truth. When we got into the cattle cars, the Nazi guards assured us we were going to a better place. The SS guards claimed we would be coming back for our clothes. We never saw our clothes again, and Auschwitz II-Birkenau was certainly not a better place.

10

Believing the Unbelievable

July–August 1944

W earing nothing more than our wet shoes and shabby dresses, we marched down a long gravel path through a bleak landscape covered in ash. Everything was gray. There was no grass, and there were no trees. We passed row after row of barracks, all surrounded by electrified barbed wire fences and watchtowers with Nazi guards, their rifles always visible.

The SS guards commanding us eventually ordered our group to stop in front of our barrack, one of many buildings constructed like a long, narrow barn. The guards told us we could enter our barrack only when sleeping. They expected us to wait in the yard from dawn until dusk, regardless of the weather. There were no sinks or toilets in the barrack, so I thought we would use restrooms in another building. However, I soon learned that prisoners had no access to bathrooms or running water. We all had to use the latrine, a large ditch on the side of the building covered with boards containing small holes. That latrine, used by hundreds of prisoners each day, was always filthy.

I soon discovered that the extremely crowded conditions of the barrack—six small rooms each housing one hundred women—made it almost impossible to sleep. We did our best to escape into slumber as we stretched out on the wood floor, packed together. We had no room to move or even turn over. With no blankets or pillows, there was only the body heat of other women for warmth. Anyone who needed to use the latrine during the night had no choice but to search for the door in total darkness, invariably walking over fellow prisoners each step of the way. Nights in the barracks were never quiet. There were sounds of crying, praying, and the terror-filled screams of women experiencing nightmares or overcome with emotion. An unexpected noise we sometimes heard drifting through the night was the faint sound of drunken Nazis singing and laughing. It was unbelievable how the Nazis could cause such suffering during the day and then party at night.

Every morning, guards arrived before dawn, forcing us to march to the yard for our so-called breakfast. When it rained, we trudged through the mud. We had the same breakfast every morning—one cup of brown water they called coffee and one slice of what was supposed to be bread. Every evening they gave us another cup of brown water and a second slice of tasteless bread. "Lunch" was different. They lined us up in columns of five, and the guards brought out a big pot of something we were supposed to believe was soup. When you think of soup, you probably think of a nourishing, warm liquid. The "soup" in Birkenau was a cold, dark liquid with a bitter taste and disgusting smell that sometimes contained a piece of a vegetable, but more often contained sand or pebbles. The first person in line took a sip, and she would hand the bowl to the next person who would take a drink and then pass it on down the line. The guards made sure that each of us sipped from the bowl.

The first time I saw and smelled this strange concoction, I joined a few other women in passing along the bowl without taking a sip. This independence provoked a Nazi guard to angrily yell, "Drink the soup! Here in this camp, you cannot say no! You must do what you're told, or else!" From everything I had already seen, it was not difficult to figure out what was meant by "or else." Wanting to stay alive, I took a sip of that terrible tasting liquid, doing my best not to gag. Even when women with infected sores drank from the bowl, I took a sip after them. I had no choice.

The Nazi soldiers selected certain prisoners and used them in different ways, including forcing some prisoners to perform sexual favors. Some carefully chosen prisoners, called *kapos*, were given the task of supervising other prisoners. The kapos seemed to enjoy their favored status and their authority. In return for their work, they received extra privileges, better food, and a nicer place to sleep. Every morning kapos woke us by cracking their whips and shouting, "Get up now! Stand up! Go outside!" They remained with us throughout the day, always treating us with extreme cruelty. The Nazis appeared to enjoy watching how the kapos abused us, and often encouraged their ruthlessness.

The kapos assigned to us, mostly women from Czechoslovakia and Poland, were often more punitive than the SS guards. Their behavior was hard and heartless, and, like the Nazis, they seemed to have lost their humanity. Unfortunately, the kapos had a particular dislike for Hungarians and made no secret about it. They complained that while they were prisoners suffering under the Nazis during the early years of the war, Hungarians were still enjoying life and wasting time going to concerts, movies, and museums. Of course, they never acknowledged that we had nothing to do with the circumstances that had made them prisoners.

We soon grew accustomed to their hostile attitudes and the ease with which they used their power. Many of the kapos appeared to enjoy beating us with whips for any perceived infraction of the rules. For me, the harsh treatment from the kapos was one of the most horrible parts of life at Birkenau. I guess we were naïve to think that the kapos would have compassion for us just because they were also prisoners.

11

Parched

July–August 1944

Although my body eventually stopped sending hunger pangs, I never lost my desire to quench my thirst. We were parched throughout the day and went to bed thirsty every night. We were so eager for water that when it rained we held out our hands in an attempt to capture a few drops. Some women, desperate to quench their thirst, knelt beside ditches where the sloping ground allowed rainwater to gather and drank the muddy runoff. I watched in horror as they gulped the filthy liquid.

The SS guards occasionally brought water into the camp, but never enough for everyone. They would empty the water into a cement basin and then pass out small cups, yelling, "Go drink!" as if we were animals. You can imagine what happened with so many prisoners suffering from extreme dehydration. Hundreds of desperate women ran to the basin, fighting to quench their thirst. Many times, serious fights broke out. Some prisoners fought each other using their fingernails, with blood running everywhere—all for a drink of water. Those who managed to get water sometimes spilled their precious liquid amid all of the jostling and fighting.

The guards found it amusing to see the fighting. I saw them watching us and listened to what they were saying in German. I never let on that I understood because eavesdropping on the guards was my tiny bit of defiance. I overheard one guard say, "Look at them. They're not even human beings. They're not even animals. They're just small worms. Look at them killing each other just for water." It was heartbreaking to hear us described that way, especially when everyone was slowly dying of dehydration.

Still, it was difficult to observe the fighting. I usually stood back and watched the pushing and shoving, feeling a deep sadness at what I was witnessing. A few other women stepped aside with me. Seeing how the Nazis looked down on us, we preferred to go without water rather than allow the guards to make us feel like we were no longer human beings. Every time a Nazi or a kapo treated us that way, it took away a bit of our humanity. That treatment made me even more unwavering in my decision to maintain my dignity and remember that I was worthwhile. I was determined to prove the Nazis wrong. I had the capacity to care and to love. I didn't lose that. They couldn't take that away from me.

Every few weeks, the guards marched us to the disinfection station. We usually had no access to running water, and no chance to wash unless we used the "coffee" to moisten our faces or hands when we could no longer stand the filth. Disinfection offered us an opportunity to wash away some of the dirt and grime that accumulated after days of standing or sitting in the dusty and often muddy yard. We were well aware that the Nazis weren't disinfecting us because they were concerned about our health, but only because they were worried about being contaminated by the lice and diseases spreading within the camp. Although I'm not sure what epidemics were occurring, I witnessed many women in my barrack violently coughing or rapidly losing weight due to diarrhea, and then suddenly they were gone. The worst part of going for disinfection was standing naked and having the Nazi men watch us. They said ugly things. We had no choice but to listen to their laughter and crude talk. After they sprayed us with disinfectant in the big shower room, we continued to wear rags. We never felt clean.

One day, as we returned from the disinfecting area, we passed a group of younger Hungarian men, prisoners engaged in forced labor. When one of the women in our group recognized a man digging a ditch, she stepped out of line, desperately moving in his direction with outstretched arms. A guard brutally kicked the man, causing him to fall into the ditch he was digging. The SS guards marching with our group immediately ordered their dogs to attack the woman who had dared to step out of line. Although we saw her fall to the ground when the dog attacked her, we continued marching. We had no choice.

12

Holding Tightly to Humanity

July–August 1944

Our focus on survival diminished our capacity to protest or fight back against the atrocities that surrounded us. Our fear was so overwhelming that we were incapable of other emotions, including anger. We had to swallow our pride so many times that it became difficult to remember what pride felt like. After weeks of living under such inhumane conditions, it seemed that many of us no longer cared about anything. Surrounded by hate and killing, we were no longer ourselves. We wandered in a deep daze, as if we were somewhere between life and death. We could see that we meant nothing to the Nazi guards and realized that they wouldn't hesitate to kill us—for no reason at all. Even when the Nazis weren't killing us directly, they were doing their best to make life so horrible that it was no longer worth living. And we had no idea if the cruelty surrounding us would ever end. Many of the women around me did their best, but they were unable to survive the brutalities we faced every day.

Although it sometimes felt I was no more than a shadow of a human being, I was determined not to allow the Nazis to destroy my soul. I did my best to hold tightly to my humanity with the tightest grip I could manage. I tried to remember all that I had learned from my mother, my father, and my grandmother. Throughout each ordeal I faced, I clung to my memories of their love. I'm thankful that I managed to hold on to my spirit. I tried my best not to lose hope, clinging to the belief that the normal world I had known before the Nazis would somehow return. Still, I sometimes felt like I was losing my grip on reality as questions swirled through my mind: *What am I doing in this place? Am I alive? If I'm alive, why am I here and not where I'm supposed to be?*

One afternoon I looked up and thought I saw someone I knew walking toward me. It was hard to tell exactly who it was because she looked like so many of my fellow prisoners—a walking skeleton wearing a ragged dress. I couldn't remember where I had met her. I tried to recall her name so I could speak to her. As I walked closer in an effort to look at her more carefully, I suddenly realized who the woman was. It was me. I had seen my own reflection in a window. Can you imagine that I didn't even recognize myself? That's what life in Birkenau did to us.

To survive, I knew that I needed to use every remaining ounce of strength, intelligence, and good judgment to make it through each day. Because I had no family with me, I also needed to rely on the goodwill of friends. Even with the extreme conditions of inhumanity that surrounded us in Birkenau, the Nazis didn't succeed in stealing our capacity for friendship. Some of us tried to keep our spirits afloat by reaching out to those suffering beside us.

One day I was able to fill a cup with a small amount of water. As I was about to take a sip, I felt the eyes of a woman watching me, someone close to the age of my mother. I was terribly thirsty, but I knew she needed the water more than I did. I handed her my cup. The look in her eyes told me how much she appreciated that gesture, the gift of a few droplets of water. Even in the hell that was Birkenau, I was grateful that I still had the ability to act with compassion. In that moment, I wasn't compromising my life by denying my thirst. Instead, I was fortifying the life within me by sharing with another human being. After taking a big gulp of water, the woman held on to me, clutching my outfit as if she was afraid to let me go. After that, she often searched for me and then stood beside me. Sadly, the day came when I never saw her again. Even if the water didn't help her survive, I'm glad I made the decision to share with her. And, fortunately, there were other women in the camp who courageously reached out with kindness when they had the opportunity—and I owe my life to four of those women.

One of the people who looked out for me was Dr. Margit Pésci, a woman who came from Kiskunhalas, the small city where I grew up. It felt wonderful to run into someone who knew the person I used to be. She was also a prisoner at Birkenau, but the Nazis assigned her to work in the medical clinic because she was a dentist. When possible, Dr. Pésci slipped me carbon pills to help me avoid getting sick. She sometimes came to the yard to look for me, and I occasionally wandered in the direction of the hospital barrack, hoping to see her. This wonderful woman cared about me and wanted me to stay healthy. I imagine it was doubly painful for her to see everything that was happening because she watched not only through the eyes of a prisoner but also through the eyes of a medical professional who wished she could do more to help. I'm sad to say that I don't know what happened to Dr. Pésci. All I know is that one day she stopped coming to find me.

I was lucky to find a small group of friends in my barrack, and we gave each other strength, hope, and the will to survive. My three special friends were Olga, a woman with strong motherly instincts; her daughter, Zsuzsa; and Olga's younger sister, Teca. We became very close, supporting one another whenever possible. I had not known any of them before the camp, but it was their support and friendship that helped me survive.

Together we endured the conditions surrounding us. We told each other stories about our loved ones and our lives before the Nazis. We sometimes cried on each other's shoulders, but then encouraged each other not to give up. We helped each other keep our minds alert by humming melodies or mentioning book titles and then asking the name of the song or author of the book. Trying to think of the future, we spoke about the possibility of being freed and reunited with our families. When we had a chance to talk privately, we frequently discussed the same questions: "Why is this happening?" and "Will it ever end?" Deep inside, I didn't know how much longer we could survive.

Days at Birkenau were a hollow existence that seemed to go on forever. Every morning after "breakfast" and then again after "lunch," we were all required to line up for *zehl appell* (roll call) and stand for hours as we were counted again and again. In the rain, in the sweltering sun, and with nothing to do, we stood there. When the counting finally ended, the kapos often ordered us to sit in the dirt or in the mud, just like discarded pots or pans. It may not sound like a big deal to stand and be counted, but the counting felt like torture because we were so weak from hunger, thirst, exhaustion, and illness. The guards didn't allow us to move out of position, even if we had a desperate need to rest or to use the latrine. We often saw women faint during *zehl appell* and knew what happened next—the guards carried them away as if they were sacks of potatoes. Even if someone was still alive, the guards picked her up and threw her on top of other bodies in the back of a waiting truck. When the guards filled one truck, they drove it away, replacing it with an empty truck. We knew if the guards took someone away, we never saw her again.

I was seconds away from that fate when I was rescued by my three wonderful friends—Olga, Zsuzsa, and Teca. It happened one morning when I woke up feeling very lightheaded. As you might imagine, we were losing weight and becoming weaker by the day. Although I was feeling quite shaky, I knew I had no choice but to line up for *zehl appell*. Standing during the count, dizziness overwhelmed me. Seconds later, I fainted and almost fell to the ground, which would have meant certain death. Although we weren't allowed to stand too close to each other, my three friends saw what happened and quickly grabbed my dress, carefully watching the guards while working together to hold me upright, doing their best to prevent the Nazis from taking me away. When the counting finally concluded, they continued holding on to me, moving me toward our barrack amid the crowd of other women. We were in front of the barrack when I slowly came to.

My dear friends not only saved me physically that day, they also saved me emotionally. The knowledge that those three wonderful women cared enough to risk their lives helped me feel like a human being again. They had reminded me that, despite the way the Nazis were treating us, I was worthy of love and respect. When I remember this, it gives me hope—just as it did decades ago. Clinging to hope kept me going even during the most difficult days in Auschwitz.

13

Smoke, Music, and a Night of Horror

August 1944

As the weeks passed, I became increasingly worried about my family. We often saw guards or kapos walking by carrying a dead person over their back. We didn't want to look—especially realizing that we were also close to death—but it was hard to resist making sure that it wasn't someone we knew. Other prisoners, also concerned about their missing family members, began to press for answers. Although we were afraid of the guards, our need to know became so strong that we asked more questions. At first, the guards just laughed or walked away in anger. Finally, one of the guards grew tired of our questions and coldly replied, "If you really want to know where your relatives are, look up in the sky. Do you see that thick smoke and those ash clouds? Do you see the fire coming out of the chimney every day and every night? Do you smell that terrible smell?" The guard raised her arm, pointed first to the cloud of ash and then to the chimney fire, and said, "There are your relatives.

There they go." I had already felt as low as I could possibly go, but this news was too much to swallow. Until that moment, I had been expecting to reunite with my family. Although the emotional part of me was completely numb, I started to shake as if I were crying. However, I seemed to lack the bodily fluid necessary to create tears.

After what we learned that day, it felt like torture to remain in Birkenau, surrounded by smoke and ash. I began to worry that the Nazis had also murdered my father when they took him away. I came close to believing that my future had vanished. It was not easy to sustain the will to live.

We later learned that the Nazis immediately killed everyone Mengele sent the other direction the day we arrived at Auschwitz. The guards forced them to walk to another building where their hair was cut before they undressed and were taken to a gas chamber where poisonous gas poured out of the showerheads instead of water. Over one million innocent people died in the gas chambers of Auschwitz, choking to death on that gas, and my mother, grandmother, sister, and baby brother were among them.

Music transcends borders, touches the heart, and has the power to evoke strong emotions. I'll tell you what happened the day we were unexpectedly taken to hear a concert given by the Jewish prisoners forced to play in the Birkenau Women's Orchestra. The SS guards led everyone from our barrack and several other barracks to the part of the camp where the orchestra was playing. As we arrived and sat down in puddles of mud, the beautiful music I had grown up with filled the air. I noticed some of the orchestra members struggling to wipe away the tears streaming down their cheeks. The orchestra played Beethoven, Chopin, and many of the melodies I had practiced on my piano—beautiful music forever intertwined with memories of love and family. The classical compositions reminded me of who I had been and what I left behind. Although I was still a prisoner, the music helped me connect with the life inside me. I saw my mother's face, smiling as I played the piano. I saw my father accompanying me on the violin. I saw my little sister and my baby brother living in a safe and secure world.

That beautiful music cracked me open, and I became aware of my feelings of anger—not only against the Nazis but also toward the whole world, a world that apparently had forgotten us. If people had spoken up against bigotry and hatred, there would be no Auschwitz and my family would still be alive. I started to cry out in Hungarian, "Here in this evil place, every single day people are put in the gas chamber, and no one is doing anything! Where is the world? Doesn't anyone know?" The music continued playing, and, although no one was answering, I continued with my questions, joined by some of the women sitting beside me. In that horrible place, sitting in the mud, we suddenly woke up. We complained. We cried. Right there in Birkenau, I found my voice. I asked, "Where are the people who can save us? Is this where we will die? Doesn't anyone care that they are killing us, that we are dying more and more every day? Don't they care that we aren't alive anymore?" The guards, who didn't understand Hungarian, ignored our outburst, and when the melodies ended and silence filled the air, they ordered us to form a line and marched us back to our barracks.

That day, for the first time in weeks, I truly wept. We were so dehydrated that we didn't have much fluid for tears, but once I began to cry, I couldn't stop the tears from flowing. I had forgotten what it meant to hope, but the music brought hope back into my world.

For me, in that moment, music was the catalyst I needed to find my strength.

After about three months at Birkenau, I lived through an event that shook me and the other prisoners in our barracks to the core. Our building was located very close to the area where the Nazis held the Romani people in a family camp. One night the sound of large trucks approaching the barracks filled the air, and we saw bright lights flooding the Gypsy camp. We had no idea what was going on, but right after the trucks stopped, we heard frantic screaming and crying—the terrified voices of men, women, and children begging for help. Then we heard the trucks drive away, and the night was once again quiet. Although the shrieking had stopped, we remained awake, huddled together in the depth of the night, frozen with fear. The trucks returned a short while later, and the cacophony of terror started all over again. This occurred countless times during the night, until it was finally quiet. In Auschwitz, everything was dreadful. Nothing was more or less horrendous, but this was a terrible night, overflowing with death. I don't know what was worse—the heartbreaking cries or the absolute silence. A profound sense of hopelessness lingered for days.

Our apathy was rapidly replaced with terror when we were once again forced to face Josef Mengele, the unfeeling SS officer who had so coldly looked us over when we arrived at Auschwitz. Mengele looked like a human being, but we knew he was pure evil—a physician who was supposed to save lives but who instead focused on killing. When Mengele and the SS officers shouted for us to stand in formation, we had no idea he was going to select women to become slave laborers in Germany. Fearful, I whispered to my friends, "Do you think he's here to send us all to the gas chamber?" With memories of the Romani camp never far from my mind, I thought, *Now it's our turn. This is the end for us.* At first, everyone tried to avoid lining up. We just weren't ready to die. Soon, however, we noticed that there was a selection procedure going on—giving us hope that perhaps this was different from the massacre of the Gypsies.

As soon as we observed that Mengele was selecting only certain prisoners, my three friends and I stood close together, deciding that selection for work might allow us to survive. Although everyone was emaciated, we wondered if Mengele might be selecting the healthiest among us. Many of the women, emotionally and physically exhausted, stared at the ground with lifeless eyes. In contrast, the four of us did our best to stand tall, hoping that Mengele would see we had the strength to work. When my three friends and I were chosen and learned we would be leaving for another camp, we joked with each other that the SS must be looking for the strongest skeletons. I was sure that staying in Auschwitz-Birkenau would mean certain death. Knowing that we were leaving, I once again felt a spark of hope.

14

Refreshing to the Soul

August 1944

The guards marched those of us who were selected—one thousand Hungarian women—to the area where we first entered Auschwitz. The kapos ordered us into the disinfecting showers and replaced our rags with real prisoner uniforms. Although it was a huge relief to be leaving Auschwitz, it was incredibly heartbreaking to move on without my family.

The guards hurried us into cattle cars where we spent days moving toward an unknown destination. We were relieved to discover the cars were less crowded than before, and the guards gave us some bread to sustain us. They again left a bucket filled with water and a second container for "sanitary purposes." Unlike my first trip in the cattle car, there was no baby brother to care for, nor the heartbreak of watching helplessly as my grandmother, mother, and sister suffered in silence. I had discovered that it was impossible to save anyone from the Nazis' cruelty, even those you love the most. I also learned that I needed to focus on taking care of myself—especially because my family was gone.

To our amazement, the guards allowed us to stand outside when the train stopped in the historic city of Weimar, Germany—a city I knew to be the home of the famous writer, Johann Wolfgang von Goethe. As I reveled in our proximity to this well-known city, bits of the past came to mind. My ability to remember Goethe, an author I admired, reassured me that my brain was still functioning. That was a big thing. My three friends smiled at my excitement as I mentioned Goethe and the history of Weimar. Of course, I wasn't a tourist, but instead a prisoner enjoying a short respite from confinement in a cattle car. The stark contrast between the reality of that moment and the secure days I had spent discussing the classics with my mother brought tears to my eyes.

Our group continued traveling through western Germany until we finally arrived at Allendorf, a quaint village completely untouched by the war. From there, the guards led us to Münchmühle—a sub-camp of the Nazis' large Buchenwald complex—where we remained for seven long months. To our surprise, the guards told us we would wait on the grounds of the barbed-wire enclosed camp for ten days before beginning our work duties. Although we were unsure if the purpose was for us to become stronger or to keep us in quarantine due to the unhealthy conditions at Auschwitz, we certainly didn't complain about having a chance to rest.

Our new barrack seemed like heaven on earth compared to our living conditions in Auschwitz-Birkenau. We no longer slept on a wooden floor, crammed head to toe with other prisoners. There were eight bunk beds in our room, each with a straw mattress and a thin blanket. There was running water in the camp, so we could quench our thirst and wash ourselves; the guards even gave us wooden toothbrushes to clean our teeth. I wouldn't call what we were given to eat real food, but it was certainly an improvement over Birkenau. Although we regained some strength, hunger was never far away.

During our ten days of rest at Münchmühle, something very unexpected occurred—a fellow prisoner made an unforgettable gesture of humanity. A girl from our barrack discovered a bucket of cooked potato skins behind the building where the food was prepared. She excitedly carried the bucket to our room, careful to hide it from the guards. We couldn't believe she had found such a treasure! After finishing our unexpected feast and returning the bucket, we decided we should check again the next day. During each of these days, the bucket miraculously appeared, occasionally with bits of potato remaining on the skins. The extra nutrition helped strengthen our bodies, but even more importantly, the gift of the potato skins strengthened our spirits. We would have loved to thank whoever was helping us in the kitchen, but knew that was impossible.

Decades later, by sheer coincidence, I met Vera Frank Federman, the woman responsible for the potato skins. Vera and I became acquainted at a wedding reception in Washington State. We discovered that we were both born in Hungary, and that we had both been in Auschwitz and later in the Buchenwald sub-camp near Allendorf. When Vera mentioned she had worked in the kitchen, I told her about finding potato skins. She smiled broadly, saying, "I know all about those potato peelings. I was the one leaving them. The first time I put them there, I saw a starving young woman pick up the bucket. A few days later, I made sure the skins had a bit of potato with them. I knew the Nazis would punish me if they found out, but it was worth the risk." I assured Vera that her courage not only gave us physical energy, but also refreshed our spirits. Our husbands, sitting beside us at the buffet luncheon, smiled to see us excitedly conversing in Hungarian. As we were talking, Vera and I finished our first plate of food, and then went together to fill a second plate. We ate and ate and ate, with our husbands watching in both astonishment and embarrassment. We then did our best to help them understand just how ravenous we suddenly felt recalling our days of starvation.

We spent our first day of work at Münchmühle digging ditches near the railroad station and loading heavy boxes into rail cars. Later that day when the SS guards asked if any of us knew how to sew, my three friends and I spoke up. The guards carefully examined our hands and eventually selected twenty-five of us to work at the munition factory where hundreds of laborers were making rockets, bombs, and grenades. I was grateful to remain with my friends, and thankful that my mother had encouraged me to learn to sew. I was also relieved to avoid the physically demanding work we had experienced earlier that day.

Our group of workers walked miles each morning and night, through rain and snow, from our barrack to our workplace. We wore only our cotton uniform and wooden-soled sandals, held on to our feet by a strap. During the coldest weather, we wore a thin cotton jacket, but still had no socks. As we walked back from the factory after each shift, people from the village sometimes came out to watch us, like animals in a zoo. Occasionally the onlookers threw bread, and we did our best to catch it, thankful to have the food.

On our first day of work in the well-camouflaged factory, the guards took us underground into a small room filled with low tables covered with bombs and multicolored mechanical parts. Although the bombs contained dangerous materials, we worked with no gloves and no masks. The supervisor told us how to insert the color-coded mechanisms into each bomb. Reading from a little black book, he explained exactly what to do with each item, warning us that if we dropped anything, the whole building would go up in flames.

It wasn't difficult to learn how to make the bombs correctly, but we didn't like the idea that the Nazis would use the bombs against the Allied troops. We certainly didn't want our bombs killing soldiers who might rescue us. Many of us had reached the point where we no longer cared about taking risks, so when we heard that accidentally dropping a bomb would blow up the factory, we considered deliberately creating an explosion. Nevertheless, we wanted to live and still hoped we might one day rejoin the human race, so we came up with another plan.

We decided to sabotage the bombs. It was a risky idea, but we had the confidence of youth and a belief that we didn't have much to lose. At first, the guards watched us carefully, making sure we did the job accurately. When they began leaving us unsupervised, socializing outside the door as we worked, we used the opportunity to mess up the bombs by inserting the mechanisms incorrectly. At the end of that first day, we were relieved when no one commented on the bombs we had so carefully sabotaged. The guards, content as long as we completed a certain amount of work each shift, were completely unaware we had found the courage to resist them. The sabotage felt wonderful. This silent rebellion brought us joy, the first happiness we had experienced in months. We had a purpose. We were finally able to defy the Nazis—with actions that might make a difference in the war. In fact, it felt so good that we began to laugh and giggle as we worked. I know the Nazis heard us; perhaps they even thought we were happy working for them. We knew that the SS would kill us if they discovered what we were doing, but it seemed worth taking the chance.

Years later, when I told this story in the city where I live, a World War II veteran recalled the Nazis dropping bombs day and night. He also remembered his relief when some of the bombs didn't explode. When he shared his story, I smiled and replied, "Maybe those were my bombs!" Although there's no way of knowing how many of our bombs failed, I sure hope that our sabotage saved some lives.

Each day we had a short break in the middle of our shift. We were allowed outside and given some food. To our surprise, one of the SS guards began to sit with us during our lunch break, asking us questions about our lives and telling us about her family in a nearby village. She was the only guard to speak to us like equals. One day, she sat beside me, balancing a tray filled with real food on her knees. Looking at my meager ration, she suggested, "Why don't you take my potato?" I was afraid to accept, worried that it might be a trick or that she might expect something in return. When I asked, "May I share it with my friends?" she immediately replied, "No! I'll get in trouble if they see I gave you food." I gratefully took a bite of the potato, but almost choked because I was unaccustomed to real food. She watched over us for a few weeks, and then we never saw her again. I still remember her kindness—a spark of humanity amid a world of Nazi brutality.

15

Stepping Out

April 1945

We worked in the munition factory seven days a week for seven months, until one day in mid-April when the guards suddenly ordered everyone to march down a road leading away from our camp. Wearing only our flimsy sandals with their stiff wooden soles, we trekked over hills and through the forest. When we stopped to rest in a wooded area, we noticed the Nazi guards changing out of their SS uniforms and into civilian clothing before they once again ordered us to walk. We wondered if the Nazis' concern about wearing uniforms might be a sign the Allied army was getting closer.

Many of us were losing strength, exhausted from the lack of food and hours of walking. As we continued marching, my friends and I whispered about the possibility of trying to escape. We were approaching a forested area when twelve of us, including my three close friends, Olga, Zsuzsa, and Teca, decided to take the risk of stepping out of line. We agreed we would run into the woods, one by one, leaving slowly so the Nazis wouldn't notice anyone had gone missing. We realized it was a dangerous plan since the guards still had their guns and were watching us carefully. We knew they wouldn't hesitate to shoot, but we were exhausted and very much wanted to be free.

When it was my turn to run into the woods, I took a deep breath and stepped out of line without looking back. What gave me the strength to run and escape in that moment? I wanted to go home. I still had hope that my father might be alive. All twelve of us ran deep into the woods, hoping it would be harder for the Nazis to find us there. We huddled together in the middle of the forest—tired, hungry, and scared.

Suddenly, we heard the sound of someone walking toward us. Terrified that the Nazis were coming to kill us, we were elated to see a tall, good-looking American soldier approaching us. The soldier, overwhelmed at the sight of our shaved heads and emaciated bodies, seemed to understand immediately that we had been through a difficult time. I'll never forget his face or his voice. He spoke to us in English, but when we didn't respond, he addressed us in perfect German, assuring us that we needn't be afraid. He explained he was scouting ahead of the approaching American troops. He needed to continue his work but promised to come back the next day. After urging us to stay hidden and not to move, he warned us that we would hear fighting during the night. Assuming we were hungry, he reached into his pocket and gave us some chocolate and crackers, and even some chewing gum. We knew what to do with the chocolate and crackers, but none of us had ever seen chewing gum and were grateful he told us not to swallow it.

Surrounded by sounds of war throughout that night, we watched fire light up the sky. We counted the hours, waiting impatiently for the sun to rise, thankful for our freedom and anticipating the dawning of a new day. We were also worried, realizing we were in German territory in the middle of nowhere, surrounded by war, with no food or water, and unsure if the soldier would return.

I can't tell you how relieved we were when we spotted our American rescuer walking toward us later that morning. Smiling broadly, he greeted us in German and announced, "The German troops we fought last night have surrendered! You are all free!" He went on to say, "I know who you are and that life has been very hard for you, but it's over." When we heard this, all twelve of us ran toward the startled soldier, hugging and kissing him. The poor man could barely breathe with twelve young women jumping all over him. He joked, "Be careful! You still need me to save you!"

Beginning that very day, I began to have a new vision of the future. I dreamed that one day I would live in America and become an American citizen. However, I first needed to find my way home and see if my father had survived.

16

Recovering

April–August 1945

Our rescuer took us out to the highway where American soldiers escorted us to an army camp near the German villages of Niedergrenzebach and Ziegenhain. We were relieved to see no sign of Nazis and were immensely grateful to the courageous soldiers who had been fighting to free us—something that I will never ever forget. We provided our names and cities of birth to U.S. Army staff working in an improvised office set up within an abandoned train car. They assured us that they would send word of our survival to the Hungarian government as soon as communication was possible.

One kind soldier then escorted us to another area—a magic tent—where we encountered the unbelievable sight and smell of actual food. After months of starvation, we wanted a taste of everything the cafeteria offered. Fortunately, a doctor warned us that we could die from overeating, explaining that our stomachs were not accustomed to digesting food. Heeding the warning, we were careful to eat small portions. However, after devouring our small meal, many of us gathered more food. When we saw the soldiers' puzzled looks, we had an immediate explanation—we wanted to make sure we had food the next day. The soldiers chuckled, assuring us there would be plenty of food available in the morning.

Another soldier escorted us to a nearby hospital where the staff welcomed us. Olga, Zsuzsa, Teca, and I shared a room at the hospital, surrounded by medical workers interested in helping us regain strength. The nurses watched us carefully, continuing to caution us not to eat too much too soon. They were incredibly caring, giving us the priceless gift of treating us like real human beings. I can't tell you how important that was. I started to fall in love with Americans and with America. We were delighted when the staff helped us exchange our prisoner outfits and uncomfortable wooden sandals for clean outfits and real shoes and socks. It felt wonderful to throw away the physical remnants of life with the Nazis. The staff also gave us checkered tablecloths that we made into dresses, and we were pleased to have an extra outfit.

After surviving so many incredibly difficult experiences—and not knowing each day if I would live or die—I found it necessary to relearn how to function in a free world. During the two years I was imprisoned by the Arrow Cross and then the Nazis, I had been completely disconnected from normal human emotions and activities. Having forgotten how real life works, I needed to rediscover everything I had taken for granted. It took time to become accustomed to the idea of freedom and making choices, to relearn how to live without guards or kapos constantly telling us what to do. Although the immediate changes of wearing regular clothes and seeing my hair grow back made me feel more normal, there was so much to absorb and rediscover. I was like a young child again, learning how to eat, how to sleep, how to wash myself, everything.

Although having food and a place to sleep was essential for our recuperation, our biggest challenge was emotional. As prisoners, we had been focused on basic survival. We realized how close we had been to dying. Thoughts of death continued to haunt us, especially when we heard many prisoners had not survived the forced marches. It was almost impossible to let go of our fear and truly comprehend that we were free. I continued to look over my shoulder as if armed guards were watching me. I was also constantly alert, worried that the Nazis might return. More than once, I whispered to my friends, "This is not our country. This is Hitler's Germany. Do they really want us here?"

The hospital housed wounded American soldiers as well as injured Italian and German prisoners of war. My three friends and I could see the nurses were busy, so as soon as we were strong enough, we volunteered to help with smaller tasks. The hard-working nurses seemed to appreciate our assistance with the recovering soldiers, and the soldiers seemed happy to have our company. My hair was starting to grow in very black like it had been before the war, and some of the Italian patients began flirting with me, reacting to me as a young woman. When I shook my head and told them in Hungarian that I didn't speak Italian, they didn't understand me any better than I understood them. Nevertheless, it didn't take long for them to get the message: I was there to help and not to flirt.

The U.S. Army liberated the Buchenwald camps in mid-April of 1945, and World War II officially ended in Europe almost a month later—on May 8, 1945. Although we were eager to return home, we had no way to travel to Hungary. The fighting had destroyed most roads and railroad lines, and rebuilding the railway system was a slow process. We stayed with the Americans for almost five months before we finally began our journey home.

The soldiers eventually told us we could send a letter to someone in Hungary. I decided to write to Mr. Szabó, a teacher in Debrecen who was a good friend of my father. I was not naïve. I knew Mr. Szabó was more likely to have survived the war because he was a Christian. I wrote, "Please tell my father that I am safe in an American army hospital in Germany. The Nazis took me to Auschwitz and separated me from my mother, sister, brother, and grandmother. Since then I have been alone." None of us received any responses to our letters, so I had no idea if my letter had found its way to Mr. Szabó or if he gave it to my father, nor did I know if my father had survived. If my father were alive and we were reunited, I knew it would be my duty to tell him the truth about what had happened to the rest of the family—a duty that weighed heavily on my heart.

17

Farewell

Late September 1945

In late September, it was time for us to leave. The American soldiers told us the railway repairs were completed, and, hoping to ensure we wouldn't become lost or forgotten along the way, they arranged for a group of us, all liberated Hungarian prisoners, to ride in a coach car added to one of the trains leaving from the local station. As always, I was with my friends Olga, Zsuzsa, and Teca. We held back tears as we bid farewell to the doctors and nurses at the hospital and to the soldiers who had treated us so kindly. Because of ongoing railway repairs, the train ride from Germany to Hungary took several weeks, with stops in Frankfurt, Nuremberg, and Prague. At each major stop, workers attached our coach to a train heading toward our destination. Although there were delays because of the miles of destroyed track, traveling on a passenger train rather than in a cattle car felt heavenly.

My journey home was intensely emotional as I pondered what

the future might bring. I couldn't ignore the reality that I was returning without my loved ones, and it was difficult to imagine a life without them. I also had absolutely no idea what I would find upon my return. Was my father still alive? Did anyone from my family survive? And what would I do if I learned I was completely alone in the world? I also realized that once we reached Hungary, my three dear friends would head in different directions, each of us in search of surviving family members.

After many days of travel, we finally arrived at the border of Hungary, an area of refuge for survivors returning from Nazi imprisonment and displaced persons camps. We left the train and followed everyone to a large gymnasium, our sleeping quarters for the night. As usual, I stayed close to my three friends. Olga, taking on the role of mother to all of us, was always alert for our safety and was especially watchful in this new environment. As we sat together on the floor of the gym, a loud knocking on the door breached the quiet. A young man entered and announced, "I'm here to talk to the woman who is called Noémi." I had no idea who he was or how he knew my name, but I went to speak to him—with Olga standing protectively at my side. The man introduced himself as a fellow Hungarian Jew and explained he had lost everyone—that he had no one. He went on to say that the Nazis had killed the woman he had planned to marry. The stranger continued, "I saw you when you got off the train and asked your name because you look very kind. I don't know if you have people to return to, but I was wondering if you would like to stay here and marry me." It was a very lonely time for the many Hungarian Jews who had lost their loved ones, and, like countless others, this young man wanted to start a new life. He had already learned it wasn't easy to start over when there were so few survivors—so he was willing to marry a woman he didn't know. Although his request came as a complete surprise, the young man's loneliness was something I would come to understand all too well.

I was certainly not expecting to hear a proposal of marriage, especially from a complete stranger. I have no idea why he chose me to talk to, other than I was a young woman and he was a young man. My hair was beginning to grow back, and I had gained some weight, so I looked a bit better than I had a few months earlier, but I certainly didn't feel like someone who would attract a husband. I was polite to this sincere young man, sorry to hear that he was alone and missing his family. I appreciated his kindness in offering me a home, but I was eager to see if my father was alive. If my father had survived, I knew he would be waiting anxiously for news of his family. So I replied, "Thank you very much, but I need to go to Budapest to see who is alive." Fortunately, the stranger seemed to understand. Of course, Olga, listening to every word, would have had something to say if I had considered his proposal. It's so interesting how certain events have the power to totally change your life. This man was offering me safety and a chance to belong to someone. I wonder what my life would be like today if I had decided to say yes simply because someone wanted me. Just like this young man, I longed for family.

After our lengthy journey, the train finally arrived in Budapest, and it was time to say goodbye to my dear friends. We embraced, wiping away our tears. Once they left to search for the trains traveling to their cities, I stood there in the center of the train station—completely alone.

Part III

1945–1957

18

Did Anyone Survive?

Late September 1945

I had no idea what to expect when I arrived in Budapest. The American soldiers helping us were unable to provide much information about conditions in Hungary because regular channels of contact were still not operating efficiently. Those of us who survived the war had no means of direct communication with our family members. Nevertheless, as survivors began returning, the full story of the Holocaust—what had happened in the slave labor camps and in the death camps—was emerging. Every war in history has had significant consequences because the lives of soldiers are sacrificed. Yet this war was different. The Nazis killed not only soldiers but also women, children, babies, and elders. People around the world were grappling with the fact that this unimaginable atrocity had occurred in the middle of the twentieth century.

Many Holocaust survivors returned home only to find that the Nazis had killed most of their family. This was particularly true in Hungary where the Nazis—after months of practicing genocide in Germany, Poland, and other countries—had become adept at imprisoning and efficiently murdering their victims. They succeeded in killing about 70 percent of the entire Hungarian Jewish population. Even after liberation, most of us who survived the camps had absolutely no idea who among our family members might be alive. I was acutely aware of the tragic fate of my mother, grandmother, sister, and baby brother, but I had no information about anyone else.

I stood outside the train station, overcome with emotion. Never before in my twenty-three years had I felt so alone—not even during my first days in Auschwitz-Birkenau. Standing there in the train station, the reality of my situation engulfed me. I wondered if there was anyone left for me to find. You might imagine that I was focused on practical considerations, like "Where should I go now?" However, my mind wasn't functioning in a normal manner. I was moving in a fog, adjusting to the reality of being outside the hospital while still reeling from months of physical deprivation and cruel treatment. Although I was doing my best to remember how to function in the real world, I was far from ready to be on my own.

I have no idea what was guiding me as I left the train station. Budapest did not look like the city I had known before the war. I simply started walking, doing my best to navigate the crowded streets. Even today, I can't tell you how I arrived at my destination—the public high school where my father's brother, my uncle Simon, had once been a teacher. I didn't know if my uncle had survived or if he was still teaching, but I had nowhere else to go. As I steered my way through the war-scarred streets, the conflicting emotions of fear and hope battled inside me. I feared discovering that my entire family had perished, yet I refused to let go of the hope that it wasn't so. I was shivering, perhaps because I had no jacket to protect me from the cool fall air, but more likely from the fear that overpowered me.

As I walked, I recalled the many joy-filled days I had spent with

Uncle Simon and his wife, Aunt Berta, before the war. I hoped with all my heart that they had survived and I would find them. I also longed to hear news of my father. Seeing the damaged and destroyed buildings throughout the city, I began to worry that the school might be no more than a pile of rubble. But what choice did I have? I had nowhere else to go.

I finally reached the school, grateful to discover it was open. I entered and hesitantly spoke with the school secretary, who stared at me with unveiled curiosity. I'm sure she was reacting to my sparse hair and ill-fitting, handmade dress as well as my disheveled appearance from the extended train journey and long walk from the station. I mentioned my uncle's name, asked if he was still teaching, and explained I was his niece. When the secretary heard this, she immediately understood and reassured me that Uncle Simon still worked there. As she hurried to find him, my eyes filled with tears of relief. At least one person in my family was still alive.

I'm surprised that Uncle Simon recognized me, but he did. We ran toward each other with outstretched arms, laughing and crying—my first contact with family since I was separated from my loved ones at the gates of Birkenau. I immediately asked Uncle Simon the questions I had pondered for months: "What happened to my father? Is he still alive?" It took all of my courage to ask. I held my breath, terrified I would hear devastating news. I didn't know if I could bear the heartache of learning the Nazis had killed my father, too. But Uncle Simon answered with a big smile, assuring me that my father had survived and was living in Debrecen. In that moment, that was all I needed to know. My father was alive. On the way home, Uncle Simon sent a telegram notifying my father that I was in Budapest. Soon after, Aunt Berta, who was anxiously awaiting our arrival, warmly welcomed me to their apartment. Once again the room was filled with laughter and tears. It was such a comfort to be with family—people who knew who I was before I was a prisoner.

Although we spent hours sharing stories of our lives since the Nazi occupation of Hungary, I didn't yet have the courage to speak about the fate of my mother, grandmother, sister, and brother. I was grateful that Uncle Simon and Aunt Berta seemed aware I wasn't ready for difficult questions and didn't ask. They told me that they owed their lives to the bravery of a young Swedish businessman, Raoul Wallenberg, who managed to save thousands of Jews by granting them Swedish diplomatic status.

I spent the next two days anticipating my father's arrival. He was taking the train from Debrecen, the city where we had lived before the war. I waited impatiently, a million thoughts whirling through my mind. I knew I would need to tell my father the story of Auschwitz, but how could I begin to describe all that had occurred since the Nazis took him from the ghetto? How could I explain what the Nazis had done to my dear mother, the love of his life, or to his beloved youngest daughter and only son? Would I be brave enough to speak the details of what had happened to them and to all of the innocent people murdered by the Nazis in Auschwitz? I prayed that I would find the strength needed to tell him the unspeakable truth.

19

Joy and Heartache

Late September 1945

E ven today, I struggle to find the right words to explain just how wonderful it felt to see my dear father. The sight of him walking up the steps to my uncle's apartment filled me with absolute joy. Almost immediately, I could tell that my father wasn't the same person he had been before the Nazis came. I could see how much the previous two years had changed him. I'm sure he noticed that I had also transformed—into someone far different from the sheltered young woman who bid him farewell the morning the Nazis took him from the ghetto.

I gazed at my father, a tall man who always stood so straight and so proud. But that day, as we greeted each other, his stature seemed inalterably diminished. He was bent over, his proud posture nowhere to be found. In my mind's eye, I can still see him approaching me as if he were walking in a dream, carrying an immense weight on his shoulders. Although it seemed he wanted to come closer, he appeared to lack the strength to take another step. Finally, he broke down. I rushed to hug him as he cried inconsolably. We were both sobbing, shedding tears of joy as well as tears of profound sadness. Although he wasn't yet fifty years old, my father had become surprisingly frail, and as we embraced, I could feel the bones beneath his clothing. We clung to each other, neither of us wanting to let go.

Finally, we walked arm in arm into my uncle's living room, and I settled in, ready yet reluctant to begin the difficult conversation ahead of us. My father, of course, wanted to know about my mom and the others. I had already decided that when he asked, I would tell him all I knew. I could only imagine how difficult it was going to be for my dear father to hear the stories I was about to share. I wished I had a way to make it easier for him, yet I knew that wasn't possible. It was painful beyond words, but I realized that I had an important duty—to tell the truth, knowing that it would break his heart.

So I gathered my courage, took a deep breath, and began to tell the story of what happened after he was taken away. I began with the details of the months we waited in the ghetto before we were marched through the city to the brick factory. I continued with the days in the cattle car, and our separation at Auschwitz by a man in a fancy uniform. I tearfully explained that I had been ordered to go to the right, while the rest of the family had been sent to the left. I shared the horror of learning what had happened to them, as the guard pointed to the smoke in the sky. I revealed what I had been told about the gas chambers and the constantly burning fires. Speaking the words filled me with such overwhelming emotion, I thought I would burst. My father sat in silence as his worst fears became reality.

As I shared my story, I realized just how much anguish I had endured. And I could see how excruciating it was for my father to hear my words. He was relieved that I was alive, of course, but at the same time, he had heard the final judgment—a definitive statement that he would never again see my mother or the rest of our family. The tears flowing from my father's eyes joined with mine—tears of grief I had been unable to shed in Auschwitz. We were both so focused on the overwhelming reality that our loved ones were gone that we momentarily forgot the pain of our own experiences. At least being together—after so many months of not knowing if the other one had survived—gave both of us strength. We were no longer alone in the world. We had each other.

Although it was agonizing to tell my story, I realized that sharing what happened was the first step in my healing. As I sat there with my father, I understood that, as difficult as it had been to tell him the horrible truth, it was important, perhaps essential, for him to understand what had occurred. He needed to know, and, just as important, I needed to tell. I had been holding in unspeakable pain, and it needed to come out. But the story wasn't easy to share. Speaking the words aloud made the events of those dreadful months seem all too real. But I trusted my father enough to pour out my heart. Later, I told the story to the man I married. After that, I didn't tell anyone else for many years. I was still too afraid, and that fear resided deep inside me for decades.

Soon after our reunion, my father and I traveled to my father's apartment in Debrecen—our first steps in beginning a new life. It was wonderful to once again feel the security of having my dear father sitting beside me, just like our train journeys before the war. Traveling with someone who loved me and wanted the best for me was a reassuring glimpse into a normal life. Most importantly, I wasn't alone in the world.

I'm never quite sure how to answer when someone asks me what I consider to be the hardest part of the Holocaust. Every single minute was horrifying, and I'll never forget the misery, the suffering, and the stench of death in Auschwitz, a place where many of the people who escaped the gas chambers later died from the inhumane living conditions. It took everything I had to survive each day. So perhaps the worst part of the Holocaust was the coldhearted world the Nazis created in their camps. Or perhaps it was the moment I was separated from my loved ones, or when I learned that my mom and the others had been suffocated by Zyklon gas and then burned to ashes. It's so difficult to say exactly which of those experiences was hardest when everything was so unbelievably tragic.

On the other hand, perhaps the most challenging part of the Holocaust was when I returned home. I was swallowed by a deep sadness as I was confronted by the permanence of my losses. Instead of living each day with fear of the Nazis at the center of my heart, my new challenge was learning to live without my lost loved ones—recognizing that I would never again recapture the security of my early life. Although the horror of being in Nazi captivity had vanished, I was facing a new nightmare—the realization that my dear ones would never be coming home. I know my father was also confronting the reality of life without my mother—the special woman who had been the center of both of our worlds.

My father and I spent our first days in Debrecen feeling incredibly lost and engulfed in grief. We went together to see the bombed ruins of our home. The whole neighborhood, like much of the city, was no more than a desolate war zone. It was sad to see our home was gone, but losing a house was truly the smallest of our losses. As I looked at the rubble, I thought about the biggest loss of all—the family that had once lived there, a happy family gone forever.

In those early days, my father kept asking me to repeat every detail—from the moment he left us in the ghetto until I was separated from my mom and the others. When I finished telling him the story from beginning to end, he would ask me to go back to the beginning. Although I stoically repeated the story, I collapsed in tears whenever I had a chance to be alone—still finding it impossible to believe that I would never again see my mother's loving smile, feel my sister's hand in mine, cuddle my baby brother, or feel the comfort of my grandmother's warm embrace.

After repeating the same story innumerable times and immersing ourselves in grief until it felt like we were drowning, I suddenly thought, *We need to stop this. We need to keep on going. We need to keep on living.* I was certain that my mom wouldn't want anguish to consume us. She had been a strong believer in living life to the fullest, always encouraging me to enjoy each day. Until the day the Nazis took my father away, I don't recall ever seeing her sit and cry or complain, even when bedridden with thrombosis. Her approach to life focused on moving forward rather than looking back. I knew my mom would have firmly advised me, "Noémi, if you're alive, be alive." I knew she wouldn't want me to throw my life away—to lose the beauty of the present moment.

After days of surrounding ourselves in misery, my father and I came to the same conclusion: that his wife, my dear mom, would not be pleased with us, not pleased at all. We agreed that she wouldn't want us to waste our time crying and would admonish us, "You both need to go ahead and take care of yourselves. Go out and live your lives." I realized that to move forward, we needed to move beyond the pain. Somehow, my mom was there to guide me, and I listened to her advice. I was ready to move on. I had already told my father the worst parts of my months in captivity. But now I told him how my friends had risked their lives to save me when I fainted and how I used all of my strength to stand tall, hoping to be selected as a worker rather than remain in Auschwitz. I described how we had stepped into the forest and our relief when the American soldier discovered us. I shared how wonderful it was to finally be treated as human after so many months of being surrounded by hatred. Telling him about my time in Münchmühle, I shared about the potato peels that gave us hope and strength, and about our sabotage of the bombs. My father also told me stories of the challenges he faced in the slave labor camp, how he had escaped, and the endless hours he spent waiting and searching for us once he discovered we were taken away by the Nazis.

It took some time, but eventually my father and I were ready to re-kindle memories of life before the war. We began to reminisce about family moments such as the transformation that occurred each week when we celebrated the Sabbath. We discussed the joy of those simple evenings—sitting together in our living room savoring the security of each other's company in the waning light of the flickering candles. My father and I recalled the unity and harmony captured in those moments of shared enjoyment and family love. Even as we mourned, reminiscing brought us comfort. Although it was painful to acknowledge what we had lost, our memories brought us strength and allowed us to continue healing.

We began to replace our talk of loss with other topics. I discovered that my father had considered the idea of finding me a marriage partner when he was talking with a friend who had an unmarried son close to my age. He and his friend decided I might be a good match for the son. I was still recovering from all I had been through and wasn't even thinking of marriage. Not only that, I was certain that any decision about something as important as marriage should be made by me alone. So when my father suggested that I meet this young man, I answered with the same response I had given the lonely man who proposed at the Hungarian border. I politely told my father, "No, thank you." It's fortunate that I was strong enough to say no to my father because it wasn't long before another man appeared—someone who had been making his own plans about my future.

20

If You're Alive, Be Alive

October 1945 and beyond

I t wasn't the least bit easy to start over after I returned to Hungary. Besides helping my father move beyond his grief, I had one important goal: to once again feel human. Having been a prisoner for so long—surrounded by cruel guards who did everything they could to take away our dignity—I needed to recapture who I had been before the Holocaust. I was twenty-three years old and needed to learn how to step back into a typical life. I needed to heal and to teach myself how to live in a forever-changed world—to find the independence to move forward without my mother or grandmother to guide and advise me. It took a long while for me to realize—to really believe—that I was no longer a dehumanized prisoner, but instead a valued human being. After months of being treated as rubbish, my sense of self-worth, stepped on and crushed into the ground, was slow to return. Although I knew it would be a gradual process, I sometimes wondered if I would ever feel like myself again.

It took time, but I finally began to rediscover the person I used to be. I'm sure other people who have survived severe trauma understand what I mean. You need to let go of the horror and reclaim who you were, and still are, underneath the painful memories. Even with everything that had happened in my life, I refused to allow the suffering I experienced to define who I was. I didn't want to make myself a prisoner of memories. I was determined to recapture the joy of life before trauma.

I began by recalling the time before the Nazis. Little by little, I remembered what it was like to experience an ordinary life. I kept repeating to myself, *May I love, and learn, and enjoy life again.* I tried to focus on the positive, celebrating the fact that the Nazis had been defeated, that I had survived, and that I was free. And I was grateful to have my father beside me. Although I still missed my dear ones and everything else stolen by the Nazis, I began to believe that, with time and patience, I would once again be able to take pleasure in the activities I had treasured when I was young. My life slowly began to return to normal, although with limits. There was the big limit of no longer having my mom, my grandma, my sister, and my brother around, and of course, there was the inescapable reality of what the Nazis and their accomplices did to millions of innocent Europeans.

I couldn't help wondering why I survived when my dear ones, and so many others, lost their lives. Although I realized I would never have an answer, the question still haunted me. Even now, after thinking about it for over seventy years, I still can't tell you why. I was young, but that doesn't explain how I remained alive in Auschwitz when so many around me were dying from starvation and illness. Maybe I survived because I have a strong body . . . or due to the carbon pills the dentist so bravely provided . . . or because I was determined to live . . . or perhaps because I had friends who cared about

84

me. I have no answer. However, I do know that throughout all of those horrible months, I tried my very best every single day to maintain my sense of humanity. That was one thing that remained possible—something that wasn't beyond my reach.

As hard as they tried, the Nazis never succeeded in stealing my hope or my dignity. How I felt about myself and how I treated the other women suffering alongside me remained within my control—something the Nazis couldn't take away. And the Nazis never crushed my belief that things would improve. I continued to have faith that we would somehow escape or that someone would come to our rescue. Perhaps holding on to my hope and my self-respect not only helped me survive, but also helped me move forward with my new life after the worst of the horrors were behind me.

21

Ernő

October 1945

S oon after my father and I returned to Debrecen, I had an unexpected visitor and a conversation that changed my life. Early
one morning I was startled to hear someone knocking at my father's apartment door. Cautiously, I peered through the opening and
was astonished to see someone familiar standing directly in front of
me. It was Ernő, my father's teaching colleague, whom I had met
briefly soon after my high school graduation. Since then, I had only
spoken to Ernő on one other occasion, during his brief visit shortly
before the Nazis turned our world upside down. Since I didn't know
Ernő well, I was completely unprepared for what came next.

Ernő explained he had been looking for me, wanting to speak
to me about something important. I remembered our meeting in
Szeged almost five years earlier, and thought, *He barely knows me.*
Why would he be searching for me? I have to admit that during the
war and after my liberation, I never once thought about him. Ernő

wasted no time with pleasantries and forged ahead, saying, "You're free, Noémi. Ever since I learned you survived, I knew I'd come back for you. It took me days to get here, and I'm not going to leave until you agree to marry me." Ernő's proposal caught me off guard, and my first response was to protest, "Look at me! After all I went through, who would want to marry me? Are you crazy?" Those words just flew out of my mouth, but in Hungarian, of course. Ernő ignored my question. Instead, he calmly explained that he had been teaching high school in Szeged since the end of the war and that he had an apartment where we could live.

I couldn't believe that this man I barely knew was asking me to marry him. The last thing I was expecting was a proposal of marriage, especially with Ernő firmly proclaiming he wasn't leaving until I agreed to be his wife. Was he that certain about his feelings for me? It was hard for me to imagine how he could be interested in someone who looked more like a withered skeleton than a bride-to-be. Before the war, when I was excited to have my whole life ahead of me, I had told my mom that Ernő was too old for me. Now, even though I was barely twenty-three, I felt decades older, and Ernő no longer seemed like an old man.

I knew Ernő was waiting for my response. Suddenly, it felt like my mom was beside me, helping me come to a decision by reminding me how much she had liked Ernő. It's hard to explain just how significant having her approval was for me. Recognizing that I would never again have a chance to marry someone who had known and respected my mom, I had my answer. This wasn't my only reason, but it was a big part of my thinking. I also realized that my past life had vanished and that I now needed to build a future—and it made sense to think of a future with someone like Ernő who was kind, intelligent, and still very handsome.

I took a deep breath, and the next thing I knew, I heard myself saying a big, loud "Yes." It's hard to imagine how I decided so quickly without taking more time to think it through. I know marriage proposals sometimes work that way—you need to be decisive. But this was a man I hardly knew! Many things were influencing me in those early days after the war. I was still recovering from the hatred, the killing, and from losing my family. I have no idea how I was able to respond to Ernő's proposal with such certainty. As is true for anyone who is considering marriage, it was one of the most important decisions I ever made.

People asked me, "Where did you find a man so fast?" The answer is that Ernő knew what he wanted. I learned later that he had repeatedly checked the list of those who survived, and once he discovered I was alive, he became determined to find me and propose marriage. The trains were not running on a regular schedule in those days, but it was the only way to travel from city to city. Ernő later told me the train he rode from Szeged to Debrecen was so crowded he had to stand on the outside steps, battered by the blustery October wind as he held on tightly to the rail. He was a very determined man.

Ernő was so certain he would marry me that he had already considered what I would wear at our wedding. To my amazement, after I accepted his proposal, he showed me what he was carrying—a package containing a cream-colored silk parachute. He saw my confusion and tried to clarify, "I know you probably don't have any extra dresses." He went on to explain that he had bought the parachute from military surplus with the thought that I could use the silk to make a wedding outfit. Ernő also offered me a pair of his pants so I could make a skirt. I later learned that planning ahead like that was very typical of Ernő. He always wanted to be prepared. I was grateful for his farsighted thinking because I had only the clothes I was wearing.

So, I thanked him for the parachute and pants and began to prepare for our wedding.

We wanted to be married in Debrecen with my father in attendance, but it wasn't possible because we needed my birth certificate which was in Szeged, where I was born. So, after bidding farewell to my father, who seemed happy with our engagement but who was not well enough to travel, we took the train to Szeged where I stayed with my mother's good friend, the woman who first introduced us. Ernő and I were married three days later. That was really something. I'll always be grateful that Ernő knew what he wanted and was so determined to find me. After all I had been through, it meant a lot that someone was searching for me—someone who knew who I had been before the war. That helped me come alive. The prospect of a happy future gave me hope.

Ernő and I were married on the grounds of Szeged's beautiful synagogue on October 26, 1945. During the ceremony, performed by a rabbi who had survived the war, I stood proudly beside my new husband, all dressed up in a cream-colored silk blouse made from a parachute and a skirt I had stitched together using Ernő's blue trousers. Ernő looked very handsome in his best shirt and dress pants. It was a difficult time, but a very special day. I tried to push aside the sad realization that my mom wasn't there to celebrate my marriage. I was grateful that Ernő had known my mother and would understand my despair at losing her. I didn't have a beautiful white wedding dress, but what I had was so much more important—standing beside me was a man who loved me with all his heart.

I soon discovered that Ernő went through some horrendous experiences during his time as a slave laborer. The Nazis took Ernő's group of forced laborers to the Ukraine, a region where the Nazis murdered more than a million Jews and Ukrainians of Slavic descent. Ernő and his fellow prisoners carried supplies for the Nazis and were required to do their dirty work. The Nazis expected prisoners to "clear the territory"; sometimes that meant picking up landmines or taking the food and possessions from families who had been killed or forced into ghettos. Ernő was filled with anguish each time he went into a house and found the family gone—taken by the Nazis—with their meal on the table still warm and waiting for them. At times, the slave laborers were required to pick up and dispose of dead bodies after the Nazis completed their killing. If there were no prisoners who agreed to "volunteer" for assignments like this, the guards would shoot a few prisoners to make sure everyone knew who was in charge. Ernő was eventually able to escape from his captors when the commanders began moving the troops to assist the failing German army. During the march toward Germany, Ernő knew the Nazi guards would shoot him if they spotted him leaving or trying to hide, but he decided to take the risk. After he succeeded in escaping, he realized the decision to leave probably saved his life.

As I began to learn about Ernő's childhood and his life before the war, I discovered that he came from a background far different from mine. My father, a college graduate and school principal, was able to provide a secure and comfortable life for our family. I was raised surrounded by books and music. Until the Nazis came, I never had to worry about having enough food or clothing. I enjoyed trips to the opera, piano lessons, and relaxed family vacations. In stark contrast, Ernő came from a very poor family. His way of life growing up in rural Hungary was a world apart from my life in the city. I had no idea how difficult it was to grow up in poverty, but I learned a lot

Ernő

from Ernő. His parents worked hard to provide food and clothing for the family, but there were no luxuries. Ernő had six sisters and a much younger brother. Ernő's father supervised agricultural laborers who worked for a local landowner, a very rich man who paid his workers as little as possible. Ernő's mother had a tiny shop where she sold food and homemade items. Although the family usually had enough to eat, it was challenging to find the money to buy material to make clothes for the children or to keep shoes on their growing feet. During elementary school, Ernő and one of his sisters took turns attending class because they needed to share a single pair of shoes. I couldn't imagine what it meant to be that poor.

Ernő was determined to get an education, so he did everything possible to continue learning. Many religious families in the area sent their sons to an excellent Jewish high school in a nearby city. Ernő and some of his friends, eager to attend this school, applied for scholarships and rode their bicycles back and forth from their village to the city each day. Ernő was grateful to have this opportunity not only to complete high school, but also to learn more about Jewish traditions and prayers, including the rules followed by the congregation's Orthodox Jewish families.

Life became even more difficult for Ernő when his parents both died of pneumonia when he was a teenager. Even so, after becoming the only person in his family to complete high school, he managed to attend college. Ernő wanted to go to medical school but wasn't able to apply due to one of the original Jewish laws—the limit on Jews admitted for medical training. So instead of medical school, Ernő went to a Jewish college in Budapest where he studied higher mathematics so he could become a teacher. To save money, Ernő took many of his classes "on the post," mailing in his assignments and then traveling to the city to take required tests. After graduating from college,

Ernő began teaching algebra and calculus at a public high school in Szeged. At the local synagogue, the rabbi noticed that Ernő knew the entire liturgy, and invited him to serve as cantor, using his beautiful tenor voice to lead the congregation in prayer.

Ernő told me that around the time we first met, his sisters were pushing him to find someone to marry. Because he only earned a teacher's salary, they thought he needed to find someone who already had money or a good job. I think they wanted to make sure that he avoided a life of poverty. Ernő's sisters spent several years introducing him to women they thought might interest him. Joking with me as he told this story, Ernő explained that each woman simply wasn't right for him. His sisters, impatient with his lack of interest, asked, "What's your problem?" Then one of the sisters figured it out. She told the other sisters, "We'd better stop introducing him to women because he has only one woman on his mind—and that is Noémi, the young woman he met in Szeged." When Ernő didn't argue, they finally realized their matchmaking efforts were a waste of time.

What I didn't know at the time is that during Ernő's visit to Debrecen shortly before the Nazis occupied Hungary, Ernő spoke with my parents about his interest in marrying me, telling them he planned to discuss it with me after the war was over. And then came the Nazis and the ghettos, and no one was thinking about marriage. I didn't know any of this, of course, until Ernő told me after we were married. I guess his sister was right—I was the one he was waiting for.

22

Strangers Among Us

November 1945

Ernő and I began our lives together in Szeged, where Ernő taught mathematics. We lived close to the city's beautiful synagogue where Ernő served as cantor. Ernő and I spent many hours becoming better acquainted and learning to trust and depend on each other. Like many other Jews attempting to recover from the horrors of the Holocaust, we spoke very little to anyone outside of our family. I don't know if the people in our neighborhood realized that Ernő and I were Jews, but it certainly wasn't something we advertised. We hoped that Ernő's teaching colleagues didn't know and wouldn't ask. We regretted not being able to openly embrace our religion, but we knew it was much safer that way—perhaps a matter of life or death if the Nazis returned.

During those early days in Szeged, my mind was still focused on survival, on getting through each day. I struggled to shake my sense of dread and to fight the paralyzing fear that had followed me since the Nazis imprisoned me. Once the Nazis arrived, we never knew what was coming next—not the next minute, or the next hour, or the next day. I think it was that uncertainty that terrified me the most. And that terror simmered beneath the surface for years. I also couldn't forget that my fellow citizens' hatred of Jews was the reason that my family and so many others were murdered. Feeling safe and secure isn't easy if you aren't sure who might turn on you. So I was cautious with everyone I met.

Memories of the way people had looked at me and treated me after the Nazis' arrival stayed fresh in my mind. I'll never forget my embarrassment and despair as we were marched through the streets on the way to the brick factory, surrounded by people jeering at us. Although some bystanders—the ones looking solemn or wiping away tears—seemed to have been quietly compassionate, it's impossible to forget the hostile looks or the crowds' cheering as we were taken away. Those painful recollections are seared in my heart.

My feelings of wariness and unease were magnified by not knowing how people viewed Jews after the war. Did people continue to hate us or wish we were dead? We were unsure where we fit into postwar Hungarian society—or if we were welcomed at all. We couldn't help but remember that, even before the Nazis came, anti-Semitic sentiment had been growing in Hungary. Open discrimination toward Jews had become all too common, especially once the Hungarian government followed the lead of Germany and began passing their own anti-Jewish laws. We witnessed how easy it is for prejudice and hatred to flourish and how rapidly mistreatment can escalate, especially when the media and governmental leaders spread lies.

I grew up feeling proud to be Hungarian, but I just couldn't forget that neighbors and friends made no effort to save me or my family—and that the Hungarian government cooperated with the Nazis and sacrificed their Jewish citizens to the Nazi cause. Although I still love the Hungarian language and Hungarian art and music, I have never regained the respect I once had for my native country. Once the Nazis arrived, rather than being considered Hungarian citizens, we were suddenly "only Jews." Instead of protecting us, Hungarian soldiers worked with the Nazis to force us into ghettos and transport us to the death camps. Those soldiers didn't think of us as fellow Hungarians but instead as members of a vilified group—Jewish people—who deserved to be removed and destroyed. I guess it's not difficult to understand why I still felt unsettled around strangers or why my fear and anxiety about who might have been a Nazi stayed with me. I had absolutely no idea who was still holding Nazi beliefs and perhaps waiting for an opportunity to continue the killing. I was certain that Hungarian Nazis were still among us, distancing themselves from their actions to avoid punishment for their crimes against humanity.

I also couldn't forget that many Hungarian civilians were complicit in what occurred during the Holocaust, sympathizing with the goals of the Nazis and willingly supporting the Nazi cause. The Nazis would never have succeeded in killing almost a half million Hungarian Jews without the assistance they received from people in Hungary. Where were our fellow citizens when we needed them to stand up and protest as Nazis forced us from our homes and paraded us through the streets? People had seen exactly what was happening. So why did so few people help, and why did so many condone the Nazis' actions? And after we were taken, many of our neighbors looted the homes we had been forced to abandon—eager for the Nazis to finish looking through our possessions so they could take whatever was left. I still don't understand how people behaved in such a hurtful way, and I wonder if they ever had regrets.

Sadly, even after the Nazis were defeated, there was no expression of compassion or concern from fellow Hungarians toward those of us imprisoned and mistreated during the Nazi reign. Perhaps people didn't know what had happened in the death camps since most of us who survived remained silent about what we had witnessed. For many years, I was too overwhelmed to share my memories of those terrifying times with anyone besides my father and Ernő. I was still afraid, plain as that. Yet, I refused to allow fear to follow me like an unwanted shadow. Living your life in fear isn't life. I didn't want to feel like a victim or have people feel sorry for me. I wanted to be a survivor.

I did my best to make sure that my fear didn't prevent me from finding enjoyment in the world around me. I celebrated the fact that I was alive, and I looked forward to the future. I reminded myself that I had left the worst of my fears behind when I left Auschwitz and again when I escaped the Nazis by stepping out of line as we were marched away from Allendorf. I also drew strength from the knowledge that some Hungarians had resisted the Nazis, risking their lives to help Jews and other groups that the Nazis wanted to destroy. It was good to know that not everyone had stood by apathetically—that some people cared enough to do something to help.

Being a Nazi prisoner had pushed me so far away from my previous existence that it took a long time for me to reestablish many of the simple routines of daily living. I discovered that many of the traditions that had once been an important part of my life, such as keeping kosher, were no longer a priority for me. Although I grew up in a home where my parents had always followed kosher practices, I learned during the Holocaust that when you're starving, food is food. In Auschwitz, we were lucky to be fed and there was certainly no such thing as kosher. As a Holocaust survivor I learned that things I had once thought were necessary, like celebrating the Sabbath each week, were not as critical as having food, water, and life. Those are essential. I learned these harsh lessons as I watched people dying all around me.

While I was attempting to once again lead a normal life, I searched my heart and my head for ways to deal with my complex feelings about God. At first, I just couldn't find the strength to care about religion. It was too much for me. It felt like that part of my life— the wonderful traditions that I shared with my family—were gone forever.

During the period right after the war ended, I didn't need to look far to find someone who had similar thoughts about religion. My father, overwhelmed by unbelievable heartache, understood completely. He asked everyone to leave him alone on the topic of religion, and I understood and respected his wish. Like my father, I wasn't yet ready to let religion back into my life. We didn't want to hear about it. We both found it impossible to make sense of the unbelievable horrors that had occurred just because of our being Jewish, and the reality that no one, not even God, had saved our loved ones. We could not comprehend why so many innocent people were hated, mistreated, and killed because of our background or beliefs.

I can now say that the Nazis didn't triumph in killing my faith in God or stealing my Jewish identity. They simply put them on hold for a while. Just as my nose, my ears, and my hands are part of me, the same is true of my Jewish roots. My faith was a guiding light for me throughout my youth, and once I recovered from the trauma of the Holocaust, it returned. And my faith remains unchanged to this day. I cannot, would not, and will not shy away from the fact that I'm Jewish. Although my views on God and religion became more complicated after the Holocaust, the Nazis didn't succeed in robbing me of my religion or my religious traditions. I'm proud to be Jewish, and that will never change. For me, it's part of being alive.

23

Different Lives Joined as One

October 26, 1945, and beyond

Ernő's determination to marry me was a blessing. I was fortunate to find a wonderful man eager to love me and to protect me. I had been sheltered and comfortable before the horrors of the Holocaust, and because my parents took care of my needs, I didn't have much practical experience. I was confident in my role as a devoted daughter, but I was certainly not prepared to live on my own. For months, I had been using every ounce of my physical and emotional strength to survive each day. I needed someone beside me, and that person was Ernő. He was there for me during a crucial time, providing the wisdom and the strength that was so essential for me in those early days.

I soon learned that Ernő's decade of working and living as an independent adult was a huge advantage, and so was his methodical approach to life. He patiently guided me, explaining how to keep safe in the changed world that surrounded us. Although Hungarian

Jews lost everything—jobs, businesses, homes, and possessions—the Hungarian government offered no assistance to Holocaust survivors attempting to rebuild their lives. And we couldn't rely on help from our Jewish friends or family members because we were all in the same situation. Fortunately, Ernő was a mathematician, so he not only had two reliable jobs, but he also was excellent at managing the money he earned and making sure we had food and a roof over our heads.

It didn't take me long to realize that Ernő was an extremely complicated man—exceptionally caring and very practical. Like others living in a world of complex numbers, he liked facts and was known for asking, "Can you prove it?" I needed that practical, mathematical brain and sensible thinking to put me back in order. I needed to know that two plus two still equaled four. And that was Ernő.

I appreciated not only Ernő's brilliant mind but also his kindness and his way of patiently guiding me. He was like a medicine helping to cure me. Ernő understood what it had been like to live under Nazi control, and so did I. And he used that understanding to hold my hand and lead me step by step into a normal life—a life that wasn't so ordinary because we were both Holocaust survivors still struggling to understand how something so tragic and far-reaching could possibly have happened.

Ernő was well aware that I had not yet recovered from the trauma of my imprisonment or the loss of my dear ones. He understood I wasn't the same person I had been before the Nazi atrocities. I wasn't the same on the outside, and I wasn't the same on the inside. Fortunately, he recognized that recovery from trauma takes time, and that he needed to be both cautious and gentle as he helped me move forward. Carefully and lovingly, he guided me as I rediscovered the essence of the person I had been before the war. He helped bring me back to life.

I had no reservations about trusting Ernő. After we got married, I slowly revealed what I had experienced in Auschwitz and Münchmühle. By allowing me to talk and by listening in such a caring way, Ernő was opening up the pain that I had been holding inside. It was a relief to be able to speak so openly. It was different from sharing with my father who was immersed in his own grief. And it was helpful that Ernő had known my mom and had seen with his own eyes that she was an exceptional person. Most importantly, he recognized why I missed her so very much.

You can see that I began my married life not only as a newlywed, but also as someone in the process of healing from trauma, struggling to unearth the secret of feeling happy and secure. More than anything, I wanted to put the horror of my experiences behind me and build a new life. In my first year of marriage, my heart was filled with so many emotions—grief and loss, but also excitement about the future ahead of us and the possibility of having children of our own.

One thing that was very special during those early years was Ernő's unceasing love. He constantly encouraged me, telling me, "Take it slowly. You can do this." He guided me when I needed it, but he also realized it was important for me to have free will and make my own choices. That wasn't always easy for him because he wanted to make sure that I was safe. Once I rediscovered my spirit, my independence also began to emerge. I discovered that it's not in my nature to listen and obey. Ernő learned quickly that hearing "no" makes me that much more determined to do whatever it is that I've been told not to do.

The summer after we were married, Ernő learned how persistent I can be. It was a beautiful, sunny day, so we decided to picnic on the shores of the Tisza River. Gazing into the beautiful water, I decided it would be fun to swim all the way across the river. Ernő had never learned how to swim and wasn't pleased with my idea, protesting, "Don't you dare try to swim all that way! If something happens, I can't help you." But I was determined to show him I was strong enough to do it. The next thing he knew, I had jumped into the water and was swimming toward the opposite shore. That poor man couldn't believe it! But in that moment, I didn't care. I wanted to prove to myself that I could reach the other side. I usually tried to be a good wife and listen to Ernő, but that day I simply wanted the freedom to swim, unencumbered by worries.

There were many times I gave in to Ernő during our marriage, but that day wasn't one of those times. When I heard Ernő say that I shouldn't swim to the other shore, I wanted to do it more than ever. So there I was, swimming across the river, with Ernő helplessly watching me. When Ernő saw I wasn't turning around, he ran across the nearby bridge so he could meet me on the other shore. He relaxed once he saw I had arrived safely and greeted me saying, "You did it, and I'm proud of you!" I'm lucky that he loved me a lot and that he was so patient with me. On that beautiful summer day, I celebrated the fact that I was truly feeling alive once again.

24

Hitler Didn't Stop Me

1947–1956

Ernő and I thought it would be wonderful to have a child, and before our first wedding anniversary, I discovered I was pregnant. In the spring of 1947, Ernő and I enthusiastically welcomed our first son, István, and were equally delighted when our second son, György, was born two years and eleven days after the arrival of his older brother. While István had dark eyes and curly, black hair like me, György had straight, light-brown hair, and blue-gray eyes like his father. Each of their births represented a joy-filled demonstration of life. I survived the Nazis' efforts to exterminate the Jews and then gave birth to two wonderful sons. Not only that, but I also have grandchildren and great-grandchildren. What do you say to that, Mr. Hitler?

I thought being a new mother would be fairly easy because of my experience caring for my baby brother. However, István was born with a stomach problem, pyloric stenosis. Although he was doing fine for a few weeks, he suddenly lost weight and became dehydrated after continually spitting up whatever he consumed. István needed intestinal surgery, and we were relieved when the operation solved the problem.

Our neighborhood in Szeged was a wonderful location in which to raise a small boy. Living near the grounds of the synagogue, surrounded by majestic trees, was like living near a beautiful park. Once the winter snow began to melt, we relaxed on the velvety lawn or strolled through the lush gardens as the flowers poked through the earth and the trees and shrubs began to blossom. Ernő and I had the same routine each day after he returned from work. I began to cook the evening meal, and he took István outside, proudly pushing him in a little cart or watching him run and explore. The quiet space around the synagogue was also a perfect place for me; there I found the peace and quiet I needed to continue my healing. Additionally, the synagogue had a spacious library that I visited as often as possible. Taking István into the library reminded me of my childhood trips to the local library with my mom.

When Ernő began a new teaching position in Budapest, we moved into a small apartment on the top floor of a four-story apartment building on the Pest side of Budapest, with a small balcony overlooking the Danube River. There was no elevator, so we got a lot of exercise walking up and down four flights of steps. We were living in this apartment when our second son was born.

Ernő and I tried to create a normal and happy life for our boys. We took weekend strolls along Budapest's historic streets overlooking the Danube, enjoying the music filling the air. Although the restaurants along the waterfront were for rich people, walking through the streets allowed us to enjoy the music played by the talented Romani who entertained in the restaurants.

Hitler Didn't Stop Me

I often took István and György to play at a park on the shore of the Danube. It was there that I got to know Lili, a young woman who had a son György's age. I had no idea that years later Lili would play an important role in changing our lives forever. I was also unaware that Lili had been a prisoner in both Auschwitz-Birkenau and the labor camp where I had worked near Allendorf. In those days, even close friends didn't discuss the Holocaust.

I discovered that it's not always easy to raise young boys. György was a child known for being mischievous. When he went to the hospital to have his tonsils out, György woke up during the night and began jumping on his bed until he slammed his head into the glass partition next to the bed, causing pieces of glass to fly everywhere. When we arrived, György happily greeted us, head covered in bandages, unconcerned about his misadventure. Years later, István seriously injured his arm playing soccer in a nearby park. It was evident he needed medical help, so I took him on the streetcar to find a doctor, a challenge because István was in a lot of pain. All the medical clinics were closed due to a Communist holiday, so I eventually took him to a hospital. When a worker informed us that no one was available to help, I said we would wait until a doctor looked at István's arm. Then I sat down with István beside me. When they repeated that there was no one who could help, I thought, *Don't mess with me. I have no plans to move until we see a doctor. My son, who is in pain and needs help, will not be moving either.* Finally, someone found a doctor, who performed surgery after confirming that István's arm was dislocated and broken in two places. To this day, István remembers the extreme pain, especially when the doctor ran out of anesthetic as he was setting the arm.

This difficulty finding medical care for a child's broken arm gives you some idea of what it was like once the Soviets took control and forced communism on the Hungarian people. And there was so much more. Communism negatively affected our lives every single day. Thinking back, it was a big thing for me to resist the Communists' authority when they refused to help István. As a concerned mother, though, I wasn't about to be deterred by their power. I somehow found the courage to stand up because I was fighting for my son. Not long after this experience, I began to wonder how much longer we could endure living under Communist rule.

25

First the Nazis, and Now the Communists

1948–1956

When the Soviets came to occupy Hungary right after the war—in a supposed effort to help stabilize our government—we wondered, "Who are these Communists, and why are they here in our country?" The Soviets claimed they were assisting us, but we didn't understand why we needed their help. We were also concerned because we knew the Soviet leader, Joseph Stalin, was a dictator. We had just survived the evil campaign of another powerful dictator, Adolph Hitler. It was hard to believe it was happening all over again with the Soviets. After everything we had been through, we didn't have the strength to resist another tyrant attempting to rule our lives—one regime that ignored human rights replaced by another.

What we were experiencing felt way too familiar—restrictive laws and angry political speeches that galvanized faithful supporters. However, this time the dictatorship affected the entire Hungarian population. Our concerns about communism increased with the beginning of the Cold War in 1949, when the Soviet Union claimed Hungary as one of its satellite states. The Communist leaders not only changed the country's name from the Kingdom of Hungary to the People's Republic of Hungary, but also renamed our buildings, streets, and plazas. They wanted everything to honor Marx, Lenin, or Stalin. We couldn't understand why, but some people liked communism and joined the Communist Party. Ernő and I were certainly not in that group.

The new government pretended to be a democracy, but the voting wasn't at all democratic. At first we had a few political parties to choose from, but when the Communist candidates didn't win, the leaders simply changed the voting rules. When it was time to vote, the Communists arrived at our apartment building, ordered the adults to line up in the lobby, and then escorted us to the voting location where they gave us a ballot with only one choice and told us to mark that name and then place our "vote" in the bucket. That was how voting happened under Communist rule. Later in the day, the government-controlled radio informed us that the person we all voted for had won—with a 100 percent victory, of course. We knew they were lying to us and to the outside world, but we didn't speak up. We knew what could happen if we complained.

It was obvious that the Communists were taking away our freedom. Yet, like so many other Hungarians, Ernő and I felt helpless, afraid to protest or resist. Everywhere we looked, Soviet soldiers surrounded us. We understood their power and accepted it because it seemed we had no choice. We were frightened by what we saw and by what we heard. The soldiers carried guns, and people who resisted were killed or sent to prison. The Soviets made sure, in so many ways, that everybody understood, "You need to listen and do as we say." It felt like the Communists watched us constantly, ready to react if we didn't follow their rules. Although Ernő and I never liked the Communists, we didn't dare question or criticize them, or share our concerns with neighbors, coworkers, or even family members. It was such a different world then, a world completely lacking in trust. Ernő and I didn't want to lose our livelihood. We needed to pay for food and rent.

The Soviet years were especially difficult for those of us who lost everything during the Nazi reign. Dread and uncertainty about who was spying on us for the Soviets added to our anxiety about who might still have Nazi beliefs. Additionally, we were still recovering from the harsh treatment we had endured as prisoners and were just beginning to rebuild our lives. After everything we had survived, it wasn't easy to once again lose our freedom.

The Communists had their way of influencing people, and Hungarian Jews were emotionally and financially vulnerable to their ways. Those in power used that vulnerability to recruit people to support their cause. Although neither Ernő nor I wanted anything to do with communism, it was not surprising that many Hungarian Jews took what was offered. People who had lost everything and were living in poverty found it difficult to resist the help promised by the Soviet government, even when there were strings attached to the assistance provided. The Soviets sent Hungarians to college to receive a Communist education and then lured them into accepting jobs or leadership positions within the Party. Communism was a mental war focused on changing people's thinking and encouraging them to embrace their ideology. That's what they wanted, and that's how their system worked.

The Communists wanted to change our whole way of life. Sadly, a life full of music, books, and culture wasn't their way. Before the war, Hungary was a highly intellectual country with many talented professionals, including gifted authors and musicians. Participating in cultural activities was a source of joy for many families. As you know, even though they didn't have a lot of money, my parents made sure I had opportunities to play an instrument, learn other languages, and read about the world. The people who owned big businesses or factories were perhaps richer than we were, but those of us in the middle class were able to enjoy very full lives—at least until the Nazis and then the Soviets arrived. After the war, the Communists barely "tolerated" cultural activity, so it felt as if the Hungarian way of life was gone forever.

The Communists also forbade all religion. Suddenly, places of worship were gone. They occupied the beautiful synagogue in Szeged where Ernő and I were married, and then used the building with its historic architecture to store construction materials. This didn't affect us directly because, wanting to protect our sons from anyone who might hold Nazi beliefs, we had already decided not to practice our traditions. Not only were we living under an oppressive government that was against all religion, but we also very clearly understood about hatred toward Jews. We were afraid that being recognized as Jewish might mean disaster. I'm sad to say that throughout most of their lives in Communist Hungary, our sons had absolutely no idea they were Jewish. István learned he was Jewish just before he turned ten years old, but that's another story.

26

My Father Moves Forward

Beginning in 1946

After the Holocaust, each of us who survived needed to face the reality that those we lost were never coming back—and the next step was to summon the strength to build a future without them. Life had to go on. However, moving beyond the devastating losses of the Holocaust was difficult for many people, including my father. He did his best to put his grief aside, but the loss of his wife and two children affected him deeply. Two of the main pillars of his life—religion and family—had crumbled. My father was struggling to find meaning in his life, and it took all of his strength to simply make it through each day. There wasn't much energy left for considering what his future might hold.

After Ernő and I began our married life in Szeged, my father was once again alone in Debrecen. Friends reached out to him, but he chose to spend much of his free time wandering the ruins of our bombed-out home, attempting to recapture memories of happier days. His colleagues at the education department were concerned about his continuing depression, describing him as a man dying of grief and uncertainty. Without consulting my father, they contacted the superintendent of schools and suggested that my father be transferred to an administrative position in Budapest. They felt it would be better for my father to have more distance from his losses and knew he would have the support of his older brother, my uncle Simon. The superintendent met with my father to inform him of the transfer and asked my father to report for his new assignment in Budapest as soon as possible. My father was completely unprepared for this conversation but surprised the superintendent by answering with four simple words: "Thank you very much."

Uncle Simon and Aunt Berta welcomed my father into their home as he settled into his administrative work in Budapest. After a few weeks, he asked if they could help him find a place to rent, explaining he wanted to be "alone, only alone." When Uncle Simon asked him if he wanted to live by himself forever, my father insisted that was exactly what he wanted. He said he would never remarry because it would be easier to go through life alone rather than risk the loss of someone he loved. However, my uncle had another plan, and it worked.

Around the time that István was born, I got a call from my father saying that he had found someone he wanted to spend his life with, asking me what I thought about him getting married again. I assured him that I wanted him to be happy and looked forward to meeting the woman he had chosen. I truly wanted my father to find happiness, and I know that's what my mom would have wanted too.

Uncle Simon had ignored my father's pleas to be alone and had instead done some matchmaking. He decided to introduce my father to Irén, a fellow teacher and survivor of Auschwitz who had lost her fiancé during the war. Once they were introduced, my father and Irén discovered they had met years earlier when my father was teaching religious classes at the synagogue. In fact, when my father first saw Irén, he remembered a day when I fell and injured myself. I was about four years old and Irén, who was a teenager at the time, had volunteered to care for me until my mother arrived.

Irén, a heavy-set blonde with fair skin and blue eyes, looked nothing like my mom, but similar to my mom, she had a heart brimming with kindness. Although my father was obviously happy after he remarried, no one would say that he loved his new wife in the same way he had loved my mom. People who knew my parents during their marriage realized they had shared a very special love. Yet my mother was gone, and so my father found another truly wonderful woman with whom he could share his life. He was a gentle and loving man, and with Irén by his side, he once again began to enjoy life. I was delighted to see my father happy and celebrated the fact that my children would have a grandmother. Irén was very loving, not only to my father but also to me and my sons.

Irén took me under her wing and always treated me like a beloved daughter. Irén's job wasn't an easy one because the memories of my mother were not far from my thoughts. Fortunately, Irén had a perfect way of gently filling the gaps that losing my mom had left in my life. Whenever she proudly introduced me as her daughter, giving no explanation, I didn't mind at all. Little things like having someone who loves you like a mother can make such a big difference in your life. Although we grew close, in all the years I knew Irén, I never once heard her talk about the war or her imprisonment at Auschwitz. I imagine that my father told her what happened to me and the rest of the family, but she never brought it up. That was the way it was in Hungary. We went on living and didn't talk about that terrible time.

27

Following in
My Father's Footsteps

1949–1956

When György was a little over two years old, I had a chance to do what I had hoped to do before the war—attend college. I decided to study history and literature so I could become a teacher like my father. All of my life I had dreamed of college, and I was finally there, looking forward to someday having a classroom of my own. Ernő was required to take continuing education classes, so we had a lot of juggling to do, taking night classes whenever possible so one of us could be home with the boys. Ernő took István to a learning center each morning before school, and little György spent time at a nursery school or with my friend Lili and her young son. Lili and I had become close friends and often helped each other with childcare.

I took classes for three years, studying literature, the Soviet version of history, and—of course—the required classes on Marxism and Leninism. I earned high marks in most of my classes, but I'm not embarrassed to say that I received one lower grade—in our required Leninism-Marxism course. I had absolutely no interest in performing well in a class where we were force-fed propaganda about the supposed benefits of communism. I wanted to do something to show my independence, but I had to be careful, so I decided to do just enough to pass the Leninism-Marxism class while avoiding a high grade.

In those days, under the Soviet government, even the color of our diploma was related to communism. When we graduated, we received a diploma with a red cover if we had high marks in Leninism-Marxism and a blue cover if we didn't. I'm proud to say that my low grade in Leninism-Marxism earned me a blue cover. Ernő succeeded in getting top marks in all subjects, so he received a red diploma. When he teased me about my diploma, I always joked, "Shame on you for doing so well," reminding him that his red diploma was meant to imply he was a good Marxist, whereas my blue cover made it clear that I wasn't doing what the Communists wanted me to do. Ernő knew me well and understood my pride in receiving a lower grade in their propaganda class.

In those days I was what you would now call a feminist. Let me explain. In Hungary, people say their last name first and then their first name. And when a Hungarian woman married, she took her husband's last name and then her first name was combined with part of her husband's first name. This then became her official name. When I graduated, because I was married to Ban Ernő, they prepared my diploma using my married name—Ban Ernőné—with no mention of the name I grew up with. I didn't like that one little bit! I was Noémi, not Ernőné. I thought, *Excuse me! I love my husband, but I have my very own name. I'm still Noémi, the same person I was before I got married.* Why should a woman be forced to lose her name when she marries? Why couldn't my diploma say Schönberger Noémi or at least Ban Schönberger Noémi instead of Ban Ernőné? One of my professors had access to the diplomas, and knowing how I felt, she decided to include my full given name in addition to my official married name. Both of us smiled when the administrator handed me a diploma that included the name I received from my parents. Yes, I was a feminist long before it was popular. My professor must have felt the same way.

I had always longed to have my own classroom, so I was delighted to begin teaching history and literature to young teenage boys soon after my graduation. Following in my father's footsteps and becoming a teacher was a huge move forward. After months of the Nazis treating me as less than nothing, becoming a wife, a mother, and then a teacher helped me regain my dignity.

The Communist government had gained control of all Hungarian schools, so, in addition to affecting our daily lives, communism influenced our teaching. Ernő was working in a national military school where the focus was on creating good soldiers. When the Soviet government took over the schools, the Communists did their best to groom high school boys to become Communist Party leaders. Of course, the government had a big interest in having as many obedient soldiers as possible, so all the teaching changed to Communist ways. Even in my sons' elementary school, all the children wore red kerchiefs around their necks and were expected to continuously sit with their hands behind their backs unless they needed to write or raise their hand to ask a question. And, of course, school children were taken to the main square to watch the tanks and military equipment parade by during Soviet celebrations.

Even though I didn't work in a military school, the governmental control of schools influenced my work as a teacher. One day I was teaching my literature class when two Communist Party officials dressed in fancy suits came to observe my teaching. As they carefully listened and judiciously took notes, I did my best not to allow their stern expressions and air of self-importance to distract me. The lesson involved reading and analyzing a beautiful poem based on a well-known Hungarian legend. I was enthusiastically discussing the poem, hoping my students would see the beauty of the words and understand the depth of the poet's message. As my class ended, the men left without comment. I wasn't in a mood to wait to hear about their views on my teaching, so I followed them, uninvited, into the principal's office. I had watched those two men busily taking notes— acting like what they were doing was so necessary—and I wanted to know exactly what they had written. I wasn't going to allow them to leave me behind! If they were going to discuss my teaching, I wanted to make sure I heard every word.

The observers reported that I was a good teacher who seemed to care about my students. Nonetheless, they claimed I had one big problem—they hadn't heard me say anything supporting Communist philosophy during my lesson. What nonsense! Of course I didn't talk about communism when it had nothing to do with the poetry I was discussing! There is no way I could have included a discussion about communism as I explained that beautiful poem, even if I had wanted to. But I certainly didn't want to! I had to hold myself back from arguing with them. After the principal and I finished listening to the observers "yak, yak, yak" about communism, he gave me a big smile, showing me that he supported me and felt the same frustration I was feeling.

And there's one more fact I must share with you. I wanted to defy those men. I wanted to say, "Don't tell me what to do!" The thought of a dictatorship coming into my classroom—watching and listening and criticizing—really upset me. They weren't even teachers, but only Communist enforcers. Thinking back, by continuing my poetry lesson, I showed them I wasn't afraid. I could have made up something that they would have liked to hear, but I didn't. Instead, I thought, *So you want to listen to my teaching? Fine!* Each time something like this happened, it was as if I was introducing myself to my own independence. I was beginning to recognize just how strong and determined I could be. And at least those two men with their pile of papers had to admit that I'm a good teacher.

Nevertheless, this kind of control was infuriating. I suddenly realized I needed to wake up. I didn't want my children to grow up in a country where teachers weren't allowed to teach freely. Despite my dissatisfaction, we didn't have the option of moving somewhere else because the Communists didn't allow their citizens to leave the country. So I began to think more and more seriously about finding a way to escape.

28

Broken Promises in a World of Fear

1948–1956

A t first, we listened to the Soviet claims that following the Communist way—embracing the teachings of Marx and Lenin—would lead to a wonderful life. They tried hard to convince people to join the Communist Party and boasted that Leninist and Marxist governments were the best in the world because everyone was treated equally—with equivalent opportunities and quality of life. It wasn't long before the Soviets took over the newspapers and radio, using them to help preach communism. The leaders thought they knew what was best for us and tried hard to convince everyone to agree with them. And some people did agree.

As time went on, the promises continued but never came true. It was easy for the people in government to give us assurances of a bright future, but we soon recognized they were telling us lies. They told us life would be easier under communism and that whatever we wanted to buy would be available. They said we could afford to take care of our families and heat our apartments. Of course, after the war and losing everything, we hoped those promises were true. Yet, the reality of communism was much different. We didn't like the real communism at all. Because the Communists took over businesses and controlled everything, former business owners became government employees with little interest in pleasing customers.

With communism, you can't have a lot of money because everyone is supposed to share the wealth. What families like ours shared was poverty. Everyone we knew was poor. Most of us had one pair of shoes and only a few changes of clothes. And the longer the Soviets were in charge, the harder we worked and the poorer we became. Teachers didn't receive a large salary even before communism, so we struggled when prices for food kept increasing. Ernő and I did our best to get by, reminding each other, "At least we have jobs."

It didn't take long for most people to realize that the good life guaranteed by the Communists wasn't so good after all. Because the government wasn't prioritizing agriculture, the stores constantly ran out of food. If we waited in long lines, we could sometimes purchase potatoes, eggs, or milk and occasionally a chicken or some vegetables. The bread lines were especially long, and after working all day, I often had to wait for hours at the bakery, hoping to buy a loaf of bread. Many times when I was finally close to entering a store after a long wait, a worker would come out and say, "Go home! There is no more to sell. Everything is gone." These kinds of disappointments might sound like small or pitiful complaints, but this kind of treatment occurred again and again. The government's promise to meet our basic needs was broken every single day.

Despite our daily reality, the Communists continued to tell us we should thank them for everything they were doing for us. The government-controlled radio and newspaper bragged about the benefits of communism, even though we could see with our own eyes that it wasn't true. I guess they thought we would somehow believe them if we repeatedly heard the same falsehoods. But, of course, we didn't trust what they were saying. We could see they were lying.

Another lie was that everyone was equal and would have the same standard of living. The truth is the government officials acted like they were way above us. It was obvious who had the power. It didn't take long for us to see that people who joined the Communist Party, especially the leaders and the people around them, had a much better chance of living comfortably. Hungarians connected to Communist leaders were given special privileges—stores with fully stocked shelves, access to modern transportation, and nicer apartments. I saw shiny buses taking Communists to work while we walked or used the unreliable public streetcars. Frustrations were growing, especially when it became evident that communism had not helped the majority of Hungarians and that the leaders were making their own lives easier but weren't worrying about the rest of us.

The Soviets were slowly destroying our spirit and any sense of optimism. We were not only losing hope, but also feeling discouraged by our loss of freedom. As survivors of the Holocaust, Ernő and I never forgot the importance of liberty. Once again, however, we felt we had no choice but to follow orders. If there was a political event, they told us to celebrate. If there was an election, they took us to vote. With the Communist system, whether we believed something or not, they expected us to do what they told us to do, including participation in public celebrations of a system we did not support.

When Stalin died on March 5, 1953, we were expected to attend a ceremony commemorating his leadership. Some people were crying and seemed truly sad that he was gone. His death seemed especially hard on people connected to the Communist Party, perhaps because they worried that they might lose their power. Some Hungarians quietly celebrated Stalin's death, but for Ernő and me, happiness wasn't on the table. I have to say, there wasn't a lot of joy in those days. Of course, we hoped that things would improve with a new Soviet leader. Given our experiences with the Nazis, however, we were well aware that things could become even worse. We lived with constant worry about what might happen next. Since the day the Nazis first appeared, I don't think that underlying concern ever left us.

We were careful to never forget, even for one moment, that we lived in a world controlled by fear. With the Soviets in charge, the freedom we had known before the war had evaporated—people were vanishing whenever the Communist State Security Police (the ÁVH) decided to spirit them away in the dark of the night. We knew that anyone who spoke up or disobeyed the rules might be next. Many times, we wondered what had happened to someone, but we didn't have the time or the strength to worry about it. Instead, Ernő and I focused on making sure we didn't do anything that would cause one of us to be taken away.

When you live in a Communist country, you never know who is a spy, who might be watching you. Many people had the job of checking and telling on their neighbors. Some of the Communist spies were paid to inform, and others only "cooperated" after they were threatened or coerced. We were well aware that some of the people who disappeared were put on trial, but they didn't receive a fair hearing with evidence or witnesses or legal representation. We also knew that some people were tortured until they finally confessed to crimes against the government and received a prison sentence. Even Raoul Wallenberg, the courageous Swedish man who saved tens of thousands of Hungarian Jews during the Holocaust, vanished after he was taken into custody by the Soviet army. He wasn't put on trial; he simply disappeared.

Ernő and I tried to quietly live our lives and stay away from any trouble, doing everything possible to avoid drawing attention to ourselves. We never talked about politics in front of the children. We didn't want to lose our jobs, or worse, if the boys accidently repeated something we had said. Yet it's not always possible to control what happens when you have young children. One day, when he was about five years old, István unintentionally sent both of our hearts racing. As we entered a store, István looked up at one of the large pictures of Joseph Stalin posted throughout Budapest. Seeing Stalin's stern, mustached face looking down at him, István commented in a very loud and clear voice, "Mom! Dad! He must be a criminal!" He actually used a word which translates to "chicken stealer," a slang term referring to someone who breaks the law. István wasn't a baby, but Ernő immediately picked him up and carried him outside while György and I remained in the store and continued to wait in the long line.

Poor István didn't understand why Ernő had carted him out of the store, but he could see that his father's face had turned white. After rushing István outside, Ernő scolded him whispering, "Shhh. You can't say that!" It was dangerous to make negative comments about a Soviet leader, especially in a public place! In a Communist country, there is no such thing as free speech, and you never knew who might report you. Knowing that government officials punished parents if a child said something that angered them, Ernő and I had a strong discussion with both István and György, reminding them about being quiet in public. For weeks, we were afraid that the police would come for us and accuse us of teaching István that Stalin was a criminal, and that there would be consequences to pay. After weeks of waiting, we finally concluded that no one had reported us, and we breathed a sigh of relief.

29

A Taste of Freedom

October 23–November 10, 1956

Our frustration increased as the Soviets tightened their grip over our lives. Hungarians who took the risk of secretly listening to the Voice of Free Hungary radio broadcasts learned that the noncommunist countries around us were faring much better than the Soviet bloc countries like Hungary. As Ernő and I were feeling increasingly discouraged about the chances of our circumstances improving, a similar sentiment was growing throughout Hungary. Many of us missed our way of life before the war and were more than ready for an end to authoritarian rule. College students, professors, and journalists began to organize discussions about political reform, attracting thousands of participants concerned about the ongoing loss of human rights. It was within this context that the Hungarian Revolution of 1956 occurred and further changed our lives.

The day the revolution began, October 23, 1956, was a normal workday, so Ernő and I were teaching and our sons were in school. Anti-Soviet demonstrators had organized a peaceful protest in the middle of Budapest that morning, drawing a crowd of thousands who listened intently as one of the leaders read a statement encouraging a return to democracy and freedom from Soviet rule. The students, professors, and intellectuals involved in the original protest were quickly joined by people from all walks of life, including Nazi sympathizers who also wanted the Communists gone. We didn't see the thousands of protesters peacefully demonstrating in the streets near the city center, but when we heard the Hungarian Communist leader harshly condemn the protests on the radio later that day, we knew that something big was happening. We were safe in our apartment when the situation escalated as protesters responded to the broadcast by toppling the huge bronze statue of Stalin in the city park and defacing the Soviet version of the Hungarian flag.

It was a dangerous time because the ÁVH swiftly began to fight back, intent on retaining their power. When revolutionaries attempted to gain control of the radio station, the ÁVH officers protecting the station began shooting into the unarmed crowd, an action that enraged the protesters and increased their determination to overthrow the Communists. The government responded by sending tanks into the middle of Budapest, further increasing casualties. Soon anti-Communist citizen militias began to form, joined by local police who shared their weapons with the revolutionaries. Unfortunately, many of the freedom fighters died when the well-armed ÁVH continued their assault on the protesters.

Because the intense fighting was unexpected, neither the freedom fighters nor families like ours on the sidelines of the fighting had any advance preparation. Residing in Budapest, Ernő, the boys, and I suddenly found ourselves surrounded by the conflict, yet we were unaware of the details until years later because the revolution, a spontaneous outpouring of emotion that turned into a true battle, happened without warning and in a country where there was no freedom of the press. We hid in our apartment, well aware of the anger flowing through the streets of Budapest and the war zone surrounding us. We saw tanks and heard shooting in all directions, including gunfire coming from the roof of our apartment building. Our sons kept asking, "What's going on? Is this a war?" We explained, "Yes, this is war, and we need to stay inside until the shooting stops." It was a scary time.

One of my eighth-grade students, a hard-working boy with dark hair, sparkling eyes, and a broad smile, surprised us by knocking on our door one day and handing me a loaf of bread. Although we were grateful to receive some food, it was risky to be out during the fighting, so I asked him, "What does your mom say about you going out to buy things?" He assured me, "She knows I'm always careful." I'm happy to say his kindness didn't cause him any injury.

As the fighting continued, more Hungarians eager to defeat the Communists joined the freedom fighters, and to our surprise, we learned we had a new government in Hungary. The possibility of freedom seemed within reach when our new leader, Imre Nagy, spoke about his support for Hungary's independence and an end to Communist rule. That taste of freedom was something to celebrate, at least for the short time it lasted. The fighting ended once the Soviet forces retreated and leaders of the new government officially disbanded the hated ÁVH, leaving us with the impression that the Communist era might be finally over. Once it became safe for us to venture outside, we saw damage everywhere, evidence of the invading tanks and flying bullets.

It was during this ceasefire that my sons first tasted a banana. In the chaos of the revolution, the mother of one of my students managed to cross the border to stay with family in Austria, and she returned with some bananas that she was kind enough to share with my family. Of course, when István and György tasted the delicious fruit, they loved it and asked for more. It was also during this respite in the fighting that István accompanied a neighbor to a nearby bakery, hoping to purchase some bread. As he was walking home, proudly clutching several loaves of warm bread, István heard gunshots coming from the roof of a nearby building. Terrified, he slowly crept home, careful to keep his back tightly pressed against the buildings. My poor nine-year-old son, exhausted after trying to avoid sniper fire by making himself as invisible as possible, collapsed on the floor once he reached our apartment. We soon learned the lull in the fighting had only been temporary, and the worst was yet to come.

The Soviets, angry about the revolutionaries' success and worried that the Hungarian insurgence would spread to other Soviet-controlled countries, decided to fight back, and on November 4, thousands of Soviet tanks and tens of thousands of soldiers flooded the streets of Budapest. The Soviets had included Hungary in the Communist-sponsored Warsaw Pact, so they felt entitled to involve their military troops and weapons in the fight. It was definitely no longer a Cold War; it was a real war, but not at all a fair fight. The revolutionaries and the new government had no chance against this immense show of Soviet force.

The Soviet tanks surrounded the side of the city where we lived and then crossed the Danube to take control of the side where my father and Irén resided. We could hear the rapid fire of machine guns and the booming sound of explosions as gunfire from the tanks hit their targets. The air was filled with the all-too-familiar roar of planes firing down on the city. The brave resistance fighters stood their ground for almost five days before they were overwhelmed by the Soviets. And then the revolution was over.

The Hungarian Revolution escalated rapidly because so many Hungarians were tired of the constant oppression and endless lies. For that same reason, it was difficult to shoulder the disappointment of loss following the courageous fight for freedom. The Soviets' use of military strength to destroy the opposition not only dashed the hopes of everyone fighting in the revolution and those who whole-heartedly supported their cause, but also resulted in many lost lives. The sad reality is that when the Communists first took power, we had not opposed them soon enough or loud enough. We had just accepted what was happening without fighting back. The same thing happened with the Nazis; we didn't resist.

Unfortunately, the Hungarian people paid a big price for their effort to achieve freedom. It didn't take long for the reinstated Communist government to reactivate the ÁVH, who eagerly took advantage of their regained power to punish the freedom fighters as well as purge any perceived political enemies. Of course, they used their usual tactics of threats, torture, and intimidation, arrest-ing thousands of people accused of involvement in the revolution. Freedom fighters and other Hungarians continued to flee the coun-try, so the Soviets tightened security along the Austrian border to prevent further escape. Everything that was happening jeopardized our freedom more than ever, and I began to wonder how much lon-ger I could stand by helplessly and do nothing.

During those days of fighting, and again when I faced the sad realization that the revolution had failed, I thought of what it would be like to live in a peaceful country. I remembered that good-looking American soldier who had rescued me and recalled my dream of going to the United States. Surrounded by violence and aware that some Hungarians had successfully crossed into Austria, I started to think more and more about escape. As much as I wanted to leave, I realized the revolution had increased the danger of any attempt to flee; although the fighting was over, the Soviets had not finished their killing. I had no idea how we could get away, but I knew that was what we needed to do.

30

Pushing Beyond the Fear

Fall, 1956

You might have had a time in your life when you were considering something important and needed a push to move you forward—especially with a life-changing decision involving a big risk. That's exactly what happened to me around the time of the Hungarian Revolution. First, I received a few small nudges, and then one large push followed by another—the last push feeling more like a jolt. And that jolt catapulted me from indecision to absolute certainty.

I think it began when Ernő and I—determined to learn what was really going on in Hungary and the world around us—began to listen to Hungarian-language broadcasts on the London radio, taking care to close the shades and keep the volume low. We knew there would be consequences if the Soviets caught us tuning in to a radio station from a democratic country. As we listened, we learned that many Hungarians had succeeded in escaping to Austria during the chaos of the revolution. One evening the broadcaster concluded his report about the Soviets' violent actions by asking, "Can you see what's going on in your country? Why don't you leave while you can?" I felt like he was talking directly to me. I had already been considering that exact possibility—leaving Hungary and beginning a new life in a country where we would feel safe.

I couldn't let go of the thoughts of escape taking shape in the back of my mind. At first, I told myself it was fanciful thinking rather than something I could actually accomplish. After all, I was a young mother with two small children. Then, I noticed the apartment across from us was empty and learned that the couple who lived there had escaped. That got me thinking about ways to get away from the Soviets. Of course, I realized that leaving would be much more difficult for us because the Soviets had reinforced the borders and because we had two young sons we needed to keep safe.

You may wonder why we didn't just pack up and take a train or bus out of the country if we were so miserable living under communism or with the memories of Nazi terror. The answer is simple. Deciding to relocate and then making plans to move, like you would do in a free country, is not an option in a Communist police state where the government regulates travel. In Hungary and the other Soviet-controlled countries, a fact of life was the so-called Iron Curtain—the rules and actions that prevented people from leaving the country. Because the Soviets realized many people, especially professionals, would move if given a choice, they forbade us to leave. We knew the Soviets had security forces along the border, and later learned they used barbed wire fences and landmines to prevent people from crossing into Austria. And we were well aware that people caught escaping could lose their jobs, be taken to jail, or even be killed. Although there was a short period during the revolution when it was easier to get away because most soldiers were fighting in Budapest, a successful escape became less likely once the Soviets tightened border security after defeating the revolutionaries.

Although escape was risky, I was finding it impossible to ignore the warning signs indicating it was time to leave—especially when worries about being Jewish became an increasing concern. After World War II, it became more difficult to identify who was Jewish because the Communists closed synagogues and religious schools, so Hungarian anti-Semitism became subtler, often expressed in attitudes or veiled comments. Unfortunately, during the chaos of the revolution, Nazi sympathizers felt bold enough to come out of the shadows to demonstrate their continued hatred of Jews.

Several worrisome events further convinced me that escape was essential for my family's well-being. At the school where I worked, I witnessed a fellow teacher stand on a table, raise his arm in a Hitler-like salute, and shout, "My dear Christian brothers and sisters, this is once again our time!" Can you imagine the horror I felt seeing a colleague acting as if he hoped the Nazis would rise again?

Around the same time, István returned home from a long day at school, trembling and fighting tears. He explained that three boys in his class had hit one of his friends, calling him a "dirty Jew." István tried to help his friend, but the bullies then turned on him, also calling him a Jew. On the way home, István asked some of his classmates, "What is a Jew, and why are they dirty?" The classmates had no answer for him since they were also unfamiliar with the term. Ernő and I had never mentioned that we are Jewish, hoping to protect our sons if the Nazis ever returned to power. So István knew nothing about Judaism and had absolutely no idea we were Jewish. István continued discussing the events at school, telling me, "I don't know why they were calling us dirty and calling us Jews. It makes no sense because none of that's true!" I did my best to calm István, suggesting that we tell his father what happened and then decide what to do. In that moment, I knew we needed to have an honest conversation with István about his heritage.

After we discussed the situation, Ernő agreed it was time to tell István the truth about our background. I spoke to István very carefully, saying, "It's true, my son, you are a Jew." Completely shocked, he stared at us, his big, brown eyes filled with disbelief. In an effort to comfort him, I quickly added that his father and I were also Jewish. Still upset, he tried to speak, but his lips were quivering. I hugged him and whispered, "Your grandfather and your grandmother are also Jews." When István heard this, he looked at me with shining eyes and exclaimed, "So there's no problem. If we're all Jews, there's nothing wrong with being a Jew!" Relieved by this change, Ernő and I told István that he was correct—that there is absolutely no disgrace in being a Jew. But knowing the realities of the world around us, we also told him that we weren't planning to tell György yet because he was only seven years old and it might be too complicated for him to understand.

The reemergence of anti-Semitism wasn't something we could ignore. You have to remember that 1956 wasn't so far away from 1945, so our memories of the Nazis were painfully fresh. After all that had happened during the Holocaust, we realized things could deteriorate rapidly, and we couldn't take these incidents lightly. István's classmates had learned their prejudice somewhere, most likely during anti-Semitic discussions within their own families. Even scarier, the chaotic political situation had emboldened Nazi sympathizers to demonstrate their beliefs during the weeks of conflict. If the Nazis were starting to stir, they might soon be brash enough to come out of hiding and openly cause trouble. And what if they managed to succeed in accomplishing their goal of eliminating all Jews? This was a huge worry, especially because Ernő and I now had two young sons to protect.

The final straw was when we found graffiti scrawled on the outside of our apartment building. I could barely breathe as I read the hateful words: "Hey, Jew. We won't take you to Auschwitz. We'll shoot you right here in the Danube." This terrifying threat was clear confirmation that hidden Nazis wanted to continue their killing. I immediately ran to our apartment, holding tightly to the hands of my precious sons. Those terrible words—so reminiscent of the days of Hitler—shocked me to my core. We were surrounded by killers again, not only the Soviets but also the hidden Nazis. It became impossible to relax or even sleep knowing that Nazi sympathizers were close by. I knew we needed to leave. This wasn't the life I wanted for my sons. To me, there was no decision to be made. The answer was obvious. We needed to leave and do so as soon as possible.

Although I had no doubt we should flee, my dear husband was much less certain. Even after seeing the graffiti, he didn't want to discuss an escape. Although Ernő knew things weren't good in Hungary, he was a planner who worried about details. He was thinking of practical matters like what would happen if the Soviets caught us, while I was considering ways to get close to the Austrian border. I have to admit I was so busy trying to make it happen that I didn't spend a lot of time thinking about the possibility that we wouldn't succeed. I was completely willing to leave everything behind for an unknown destination and unknown way of life and, I admit, to put all of us in danger to get there. Although I knew it would be risky, I believed it was the only way to keep our family safe.

I was convinced we should try to escape, and I just wouldn't let it go. During that time in Europe, a good wife was supposed to agree with her husband, just for the peace that comes with allowing the husband to be in charge. Ernő was smart and reasonable, so I was usually compliant and didn't cause problems. And I did that for many years without complaining. Life was easier that way. Although I had gone along with many things during our marriage, this was so important that I just wasn't going to give up. And I didn't have the luxury of waiting patiently for Ernő to agree with me. I couldn't remain silent when I was so certain that we should leave immediately. I saw no other option, and nothing was going to change my mind. I had to do everything possible to convince Ernő to support my decision.

Ernő and I had many conversations about whether or not it was safe to leave. We talked about it every night after the boys went to sleep. With my dear husband, I had learned to be strategic in my approach. In this situation, compromise was not an option, so day after day I persisted, continuing the same conversation: "We need to go. We can't stay here." I argued that we had no choice—we should attempt an escape and do it soon. Ernő would ask, "Do you know what you're proposing? Do you understand what you're asking us to do? Maybe they'll find us and report us to the secret police. Or maybe they'll do something much worse—kill us all." And I would answer, "Yes, I understand exactly what I'm saying. And we need to go!" Ernő would explain, "We have a home here. I know life is hard, but at least we're alive." And he would patiently continue, "I understand your concerns, but I have one big problem with your idea. I'm not willing to put our sons in danger." Then he would repeat the perils we would face, and each time I would respond by asking, "Aren't we putting the boys in danger by staying?" Finally, at my wit's end, I told Ernő that he could stay if he wanted to, but that I was going to escape with the boys, whether he liked it or not.

I now understand why Ernő was so opposed to the idea of attempting to flee. I was asking Ernő to leave everything familiar and jump into the unknown. I understand why that frightened him. He had survived the Holocaust, and although his life wasn't easy under the Communists, at least it felt settled. Ernő loved our sons and wanted to keep them safe. He was the husband and the father—the one in charge of protecting us. The last thing he wanted was to risk endangering his family, especially when there was no proof we would succeed.

I knew I was making progress when Ernő started to look beyond the dangers and began to ask practical questions, like "How will we get across the border, and where will we go?" or "Where will we sleep, and what will we give the boys to eat?" Although I didn't have answers to his questions, I kept giving him the same response, "We'll somehow figure it out." And finally, Ernő agreed. He finally understood that the only way to keep our sons safe and free was to leave Hungary! From that moment on, I didn't need to spend any more energy trying to convince Ernő. But that presented a new challenge: finding a way for us to safely escape.

31

A Chance and a Warning

Late November 1956

As soon as Ernő and I made the decision to escape, fleeing the country was all I could think about. Suddenly there was hope, and my attention turned to figuring out a plan. I understood we would be leaving behind my father and Irén, but at the same time we would be breaking away from the horrors of the Holocaust and the Communists controlling our every move. I was ready to close that door. I longed for a country where we could live without fear. The Hungarian government had turned against us once already, and I didn't trust that it wouldn't happen again. I also couldn't shake the feeling that the Nazis were feeling stronger and just waiting to rise from the shadows.

I was very much in this mood of believing we needed to go when I learned of a possible way to escape. One evening, Ernő and I were listening to the London radio when the Hungarian-speaking reporter mentioned that a train conductor was willing to take passengers close to the Austrian border. The conductor, wanting to escape and willing to help others, planned to commandeer the train and proceed past the security guards at the border inspection station without stopping. The broadcast didn't mention the particular train or station but gave some details that made me guess that it was the station in our area of the city. Ernő and I made the decision to leave with the boys early the next morning to see if we could locate the train.

We walked to the station before dawn, determined to find the train mentioned in the radio broadcast. We left with only the clothes on our backs. However, aware we would have a long walk through the snow, we bundled up, wearing several layers of clothes beneath our coats. Instead of telling the boys we were planning to escape, we explained we needed to dress warmly because we were taking the train to visit a friend outside the city. I don't recall exactly how we located the correct train but, somehow, we did. Although Ernő and I were nervous, the boys, knowing nothing about our plan to escape or the risk we were taking, were excited about riding the train. Once we settled into our seats, István looked at a woman sitting close to us and asked, "Are you wearing extra clothes like we are?" Ernő and I quickly said, "Shhhh," but a while later György, very curious like so many seven-year-old boys, loudly inquired, "Mom, why does everyone have on so many clothes?"

As the train moved toward the Austrian border, a man entered the train car to share some discouraging news—the plan to take the train close to the border wasn't going to work. He explained the conductor received a warning that the Soviets knew about the attempted escape. Given this new information, the conductor stopped the train and told everyone to exit. Along with the other disappointed passengers, we were left in a snowy field. I honestly can't remember what happened to the conductor or the train. My focus was on my sons and what might happen next.

We were in the middle of nowhere, but, as a group, we headed in the direction of the Austrian border. We walked in the freezing temperatures for what seemed like hours before spotting some Soviet border guards riding toward us on horseback. Our sons, excited to see the soldiers in their fancy uniforms, didn't understand the danger until the soldiers began yelling "You're not going anywhere!" When some of the soldiers began firing their guns into the air, apparently wanting to scare us, the boys grabbed our hands and held tightly, their excitement suddenly replaced with fear. Some of the passengers tried giving explanations about traveling to visit relatives close to the border, but of course, the Soviets knew why we were on that train. The soldiers herded us toward some large haystacks next to the road and ordered us to wait there, closely guarding us each step of the way. In the early morning hours, a government bus arrived to take us away from the border and back to the city.

When we arrived in Budapest, the soldiers ordered the men to go with them but allowed the women and children to leave. I held tightly to István and György as we walked through the dark streets, eager to get home and out of the bitter cold. Before we left, we had asked my father to stay in our apartment in case the Soviets forced us to return. Because of the shortage of apartments in Budapest, people often waited in the street, watching to see who was coming and going, quickly moving into a vacant apartment. For the same reason, Irén had remained home, ensuring that their apartment wasn't taken over by strangers. As I slowly climbed the four flights of stairs, feeling discouraged and anxious about what was happening with Ernő, I was grateful my father was waiting for us. When he opened the door, immediately sensing my disappointment and worry, he hugged me and whispered, "One of my eyes is smiling because I can see you again, but my other eye is crying because you were forced to return."

When they took Ernő away I didn't know how they might punish him, so I was tremendously relieved when he returned to the apartment later that morning. Although they didn't put Ernő in jail, he came back with a very stern message from the Soviets: "Tell your family that we know you want to leave. You will be watched. You won't know who is watching, but we will be watching. We don't have enough jail space for you and your family, but you should be in jail. Don't you dare try to leave again!"

The threat was intended to scare us, but for me it had the opposite effect. I was even more determined to leave, furious that the Soviets dared to tell us what they would allow us to do or not do. I thought, *No one is going to take away my freedom!* In contrast, Ernő, who had been the recipient of the harsh warning, felt we should obey. But that wasn't acceptable to me. My anger spurred me to action. I knew we had no choice; we needed to try again, making sure that next time we succeeded. I turned to my dear husband—who the Soviets had just reprimanded for taking a risk I had pushed him to take—and said, "Ernő, we survived the Holocaust. We got married, and we had children, and those Soviet soldiers are giving us orders about what we can do or cannot do. I refuse to listen. We are going. If we wanted to go yesterday, with this warning, we now need to go more than ever. How dare they tell us not to go!" I was furious and didn't have the energy to pretend otherwise.

It was incredibly disappointing that we were discovered so close to the border. Yet I refused to give up. Even with the warning, my only thought was, *We will go, and you won't stop us.* I heard the threat that the Soviets had delivered—loud and clear—but I refused to listen. I had lost loved ones during the Holocaust; I just couldn't risk that happening again. I wasn't known to be a forceful woman, but apparently, when it was needed, I became that woman. The lessons I had learned in the Holocaust were pushing me forward, and I was determined to succeed.

32

A Perilous Path to Freedom

December 28–29, 1956

Swallowing my disappointment after our unsuccessful attempt to escape on the train, I concentrated on coming up with another plan about how to cross the border. Ernő and I continued to listen to the British radio, and I was dismayed to hear that fewer people were successfully escaping. Although I was discouraged, my certainty that we needed to get away never faded. I didn't know how we would do it, but I refused to give up on the idea of leaving. That's when my good friend Lili came to the rescue. She realized how strongly I felt about leaving Hungary. Being a mother herself, she understood my determination to protect my sons, and we had often whispered to each other about ways to escape. Concerned about the violence and lack of human rights in Hungary, Lili and I both wanted our children to have a chance to grow up in a free country. Lili's husband was reluctant to even discuss the topic, however, and she had no luck changing his mind.

Lili knew how distressed I was about our failed escape and understood my anger at the threats the Soviets made to Ernő. It wasn't long before she shared a new idea, explaining that the factory where she worked often transported wool, cotton, and other textiles to another factory on the outskirts of Sopron, a Hungarian city about five kilometers from the Austrian border. Lili had heard that one of the assistant drivers intended to escape with his wife and young daughter and suggested that perhaps we could hide with his family in one of their shipments. She asked, "If I get permission for you to hide with the goods we're shipping, will you do it?" I didn't hesitate, replying, "Of course we'd go!" I was delighted to learn a few days later that her employer had approved of the plan.

When I shared the idea with Ernő, he wasn't excited about the prospect of hiding and risking discovery by the Soviets, explaining he loved us and didn't want to put us in danger of severe punishment. I once again repeated, "That's why we need to go." For Ernő it wasn't easy to agree to another escape attempt, especially after the stern warning he had received. Although I was ten years younger than my husband, as I tried to convince him, it seemed more like a twenty-year difference between us. He was digging in his heels because he didn't want to put our lives in danger, yet he also knew he didn't have much choice because I wasn't going to give up. He finally agreed.

Honestly, it wasn't easy for me either because I clearly understood the danger we were facing, especially if the Soviets caught us again. I know that Ernő's tremendous love for me helped him make the decision to give in. And I give him a lot of credit. Once he agreed, he never complained. Even when we were in dangerous situations as we carried out the plan, he never once blamed me or said, "I told you so."

A Perilous Path to Freedom

Of course, we were careful to avoid talking about escaping in front of the boys. It wasn't safe. If they accidentally mentioned we were planning to leave, we could have been in serious trouble. It was important for István and György to stay calm and quiet as we traveled for hours hidden in the back of a truck, but at the same time I didn't want them to be afraid. So I did my best to make our escape seem like a big adventure, while also making sure they understood we would have no bathroom, no water, and no food. I also told them that while we were in the truck, we would need to be completely silent.

And then I made some promises. Wanting to help the boys envision the rewards at the end of the journey, I mentioned we would buy each of them a little toy car—something they had only dreamed of because our income barely provided for food and rent. I also enticed them by mentioning the food we could buy when we reached our destination, such as the banana they had recently tasted, promising them, "When we get to America, we will all get a banana." Then I added the possibility of oranges, something the boys had seen but never tasted. And I concluded with the promise of one more wonderful treat—chocolate. When I asked, "Do you want to go?" they both eagerly nodded their agreement.

We didn't know the exact details of the plan but were told to meet at the local factory early in the morning of December 28, 1956. Once again, we left with the clothes on our backs and a small amount of food, nothing more. With my father once again guarding our apartment, we walked briskly through the snowy streets toward the factory dressed in layers of our warmest clothes. When we arrived, the truck was already loaded with a small opening in the wool, barely large enough for us to squeeze inside. We carefully maneuvered into the shipment, finding the wife and two-year-old daughter of the driver's assistant already concealed in the small enclosure—all of us completely hidden. As I sat with György on my lap and István squeezed tightly against Ernő, the driver sealed the opening. Our hiding space amid the wool was so compact that we could barely move. I took deep breaths, trying to push aside the sensation that we might all suffocate.

The trip from Budapest to Sopron would normally take about three or four hours, but it took us much longer because of the snowy roads and multiple stops. The Soviets knew people were trying to escape, so we had prepared the boys for the many inspections along the way, reminding them that we needed to remain silent and suggesting they pretend to have tape over their mouths. As we bumped along the snowy roads, György and István sat quietly just as they had promised. They didn't complain about not having food, water, or a bathroom. Although everyone had been unhappy when I said we couldn't drink coffee or water before we left the apartment, it certainly helped when we had so many hours to travel. Looking back, I have no idea how those two little boys did everything we needed them to do during that uncomfortable ride.

Many times along the way, Soviet soldiers stopped the truck to review the official paperwork authorizing the driver and his helper to leave Budapest and travel to Sopron. During the first few stops, we heard Hungarian soldiers checking the paperwork, but as we got closer to the border, the checkpoints became more frequent, and we could hear the soldiers speaking Russian. With each stop, we shivered in fear, wondering if the soldiers would discover us and, if so, what they would do. Even one sound could have jeopardized us, but István, György, and the young girl were quiet the entire journey. During our last inspection, after hearing Russians approach the truck, we felt something sharp poking into our hiding place—guards using their bayonets in an attempt to detect anyone concealed inside the textiles. Feeling the bayonet just inches away, I held György tightly against me, my heart pounding. György still remembers the bayonet almost hitting his nose.

It was a huge relief when we reached our final stop, the factory in Sopron. No one saw us emerge from our hiding place except the factory manager who was expecting our arrival. We were cold and tired and hungry, our joints stiff from hours of sitting in a cramped position. Apologizing for having no food to offer us, the manager showed us an empty room where we could spend the night, explaining that a local farmer who had a side business helping people cross the border would come for us in the morning. Knowing we had a long journey ahead of us, we did our best to sleep, huddling with the boys on the cold floor. We waited until dawn, and then it was time for us to meet our guide.

The farmer appeared before daybreak, asking if we were ready to leave for Austria. Having no knowledge of the area, Ernő and I, as well as the driver's assistant and his wife, were grateful to have the farmer lead the way. It wasn't easy to put our lives and the lives of our sons into the hands of someone we didn't know—especially during a time when people spied for the Communists and reported on people trying to escape. The farmer asked for half of our Hungarian money before we left, explaining that we would pay him the remainder just before we crossed the border. Aware that Hungarian money would be of no use in Austria and desperate to escape, we agreed to his terms. In that situation, you don't argue.

We plodded along after the farmer, not sure how long it would take us to reach Austria, especially because we were avoiding the main road and, therefore, trudging through very deep snow. The morning was bright, and everywhere we looked, the snowy landscape glistened. The air was brisk, and we became increasingly chilled as we went up in elevation and the wind increased. We were grateful that we were dressed warmly, wearing ankle-high boots and warm woolen socks. Although the boys and Ernő had on several pairs of pants, my legs were freezing because I was wearing a skirt, which was the custom for women in those days. At least we all had coats and the scarves and hats I had crocheted for each of us.

The farmer explained he was taking us to an area out of sight of the guard towers, but warned us to remain silent to avoid detection by soldiers hidden in the forest. At one point, as we were maneuvering through deep snow with the wind howling and snow blowing around us, the young girl began screaming. I didn't blame her at all. We were all hungry and tired and cold. And, of course, she was too young to understand why we were outside in the strong wind. Fortunately, because it was such a blustery day, the sound of the wind roaring through the trees drowned out her cries.

We knew we had arrived at the border when we saw a strip of land—a no man's land about a hundred yards wide—where trees had been cut away. The cleared area was strewn with uneven piles of bricks covered by snow. The farmer asked for his money and then pointed us in the correct direction, warning us, "Be careful. Border guards might be hiding in the trees, and you don't know who is watching from up on the mountain. Be sure to continue in the direction I pointed so you don't accidentally walk toward the watchtowers or cross back into Hungary." And then he wished us luck and walked away, leaving us alone in the snowy wilderness.

I told György and István to cross the obstacle-filled border first, assuring them we would be right behind them. The boys were able to manage the uneven terrain without difficulty, and they were soon standing in Austria. István remembers wondering in that instant, *What will I do if my parents don't get here? How will I take care of my little brother?* However, those thoughts were fleeting because Ernő and I, following close behind and doing our best to keep our footing as we maneuvered around the bricks, were soon exchanging hugs with our sons. We had made it to Austria.

33

Finally Free?

December 29, 1956

W hat had I gotten us into? The other family had already disappeared into the forest, so we were alone in the middle of nowhere. We had no food and no money, and nothing more than the clothes we were wearing. Although we were relieved to have arrived safely in Austria, we had a long walk ahead of us and were unsure of our destination. All we could do was trudge forward in the direction the farmer pointed, doing our best to avoid crossing back into Hungary. Concerned that Soviet soldiers or spies might spot us, we kept looking over our shoulders to make sure no one was following us.

Soon after we crossed the border, Ernő wanted to stop and rest. I didn't blame him. It had been a difficult hike, traveling up and down the foothills in deep snow and in bitter cold. And Ernő and I were city people unfamiliar with hiking in the mountains. Fortunately, the boys were intrigued by the idea of escaping the bad guys and spurred on by the excitement of our journey, so they weren't complaining. And I was fueled by adrenaline, a mother intent on helping my sons find shelter before nightfall. I was also concerned that we hadn't ventured far enough from the Hungarian border, and I didn't want to take the risk of being discovered and forced back to Hungary. We needed to cover as much ground as possible before dark, so I insisted we continue walking.

Despite my concerns, Ernő soon decided he was done with walking and began insisting, "I can't go on. I'm tired. I need to rest, just for a minute." If Ernő sat down, I doubted he would be able to get up again. It was below freezing outside, so it would be dangerous, perhaps even fatal, to stop. Ernő's eyes were glazed, and his face was extremely pale—as white as the snow that surrounded us. I recognized the peril of stopping and resting, especially because Ernő wasn't thinking clearly. Normally, in our family, what Ernő said was the word we followed, but this situation required me to take charge. I had no doubt that we would have a big problem if Ernő succumbed to cold and exhaustion, but I didn't have much time to think of a plan.

I decided if we could make Ernő angry, it might get his circulation going. So I enlisted our sons' help, saying, "Boys, I want you to figure out a way to make your dad really, really mad." István and György looked at me, totally confused, wondering why I would ask them to upset their father. They couldn't believe what I was asking. Both boys could see Ernő was exhausted but thought he just needed to rest. I continued to insist, "Hurry! Get Dad as angry as you can!" The boys remember hoping that I knew what I was doing because they were sure that Ernő would be furious with them. When I remained adamant, they decided to comply.

István and György did exactly as I had requested—they started making fun of Ernő, saying anything they could think of to upset him. Then they threw snowballs at him, causing his hat to fall off. It worked. Ernő was no longer asking to sit down. Before long, his coloring returned to normal, and his face then turned beet red. I said, "Just keep throwing!" wanting to make sure that Ernő was able to think clearly again. And the very second I said, "That's enough now," the boys immediately stopped. Even though Ernő gave me a look that said, "I know what you were up to," I quickly explained that the boys were just following my instructions. When Ernő started to laugh, it was a relief for all of us. Then he gave each of us a big hug, and we continued our trek through the snow.

We were in a lovely part of Austria, with beautiful mountains and snow-covered evergreens. Nevertheless, my only focus that day was on ensuring our safety by finding food and shelter. As we walked up the mountain and the snow became deeper, the boys continued to treat our hike as an enjoyable outing. Ernő and I did our best to avoid falling as we carefully maneuvered in the deep snow while the boys raced ahead of us.

István and György eventually began complaining they were hungry, but I had nothing to give them, so I picked up a handful of snow and asked, "I know this is snow, but it looks like ice cream, doesn't it? Why don't we pretend? Here's some delicious ice cream. Would you like some?" Of course, they wanted real food and weren't easy to convince, but they gave it a try and began taking bits of snow and pretending it was ice cream. Later, when I heard, "Mom, I'm thirsty," I answered, "I know this is snow, but it could be water!" And when the boys said, "I have to go to the bathroom!" I couldn't resist joking, "Go for it, boys! Go out in the snow and do what you need to do, but don't mess up my dinner!" It felt good to laugh.

We continued trudging through the snow until we came to a cemetery marked with a sign written in German. I was so relieved that I exclaimed, "Look! A cemetery!" in a tone of total excitement. My sons looked at me with concern, wondering why I was so happy to see a cemetery. I explained, "If dead people are buried here, we must be close to people who are alive. If people live nearby, we must be close to food and shelter." The boys eagerly walked ahead, hoping to be the first to spot civilization.

Not far beyond the cemetery, we came to a small town, and in the center of the village square, we were greeted by the twinkling lights of a Christmas tree brilliantly reflecting on the glistening snow, looking like a Christmas postcard come to life. We couldn't believe what we were seeing! That magical tree felt like a welcoming beacon of hope. And to our amazement, there was an International Red Cross shelter right in the center of the village. A woman stepped out of the building, and seeing our shivering sons, she grabbed the boys without a word, rushing them up the hill and into the shelter. Ernő and I plodded slowly behind. Entering the warm house, we found the boys sitting on a bed happily sipping hot chocolate. Their ice-covered clothes had been removed, and they were bundled in thick pajamas. György looked up at me and asked, "Is this America, Mom?" Still concerned about being discovered, I quietly warned him to stay quiet. I had noticed a young man dressed for travel outside the shelter, and his presence worried me, especially after hearing there were spies on the Austrian side of the border. I spoke very little beyond thanking the woman for giving us food and allowing us to stay the night. I did my best to put my concern about the young man aside and focus on my relief that we had made it to Austria and found shelter for the night.

So that's how we made the freezing journey out of Hungary and finally escaped Soviet domination. I didn't know what we would do the next day, but I was thankful that we were not only safe but also free. If you look at our situation, or the story of my life, you see a lot of danger. But each time I faced danger—every single time—I somehow got out of it. I don't know why that is, but I'm grateful that I was able to keep moving forward, believing that I would succeed if I didn't give up. It's not a small thing that we escaped from Hungary and found shelter on that dark, snowy night.

34

Helpful Hands

December 30, 1956–January 1957

W e woke up early the next morning, eager to continue toward Vienna, the capital of Austria, where we hoped to receive permission to travel to America. István and György were happy to find that their clothes, warmed by the fire, were no longer wet. Ernő and I, having slept in our wet clothes, were also thankful to be dry. The woman managing the shelter kindly offered us something to eat and drink before we once again bundled up and confronted the bitter cold.

We were relieved to see that the young man who had been outside the night before was already gone. We hoped he was a refugee and not a spy, but we knew how the Communist police state worked and had heard about informers in civilian clothing looking for Hungarians who had escaped. And when the young man disappeared, the question became, "Where did he go?" Keeping him in mind, we left quickly and remained alert as we looked for the bus we learned would take us to a nearby city. Once there, someone directed us to an elementary school where relief workers were providing food and shelter in the school gymnasium. Although we were eager to keep moving, we had no money and no idea where we would find our next meal, so we tried to relax and enjoy the dinner provided at the shelter. I shared our story with one of the workers and mentioned how I had promised my sons a toy after we completed our journey. To my astonishment, someone later appeared with gifts for István and György—two shiny buses, each the size of a shoebox. We spent the night huddled together on the cold gym floor surrounded by other Hungarian refugees. We arose early the next morning ready to move on, with the boys happily clutching their new toys.

Someone directed us to a bus headed for Vienna, and we were relieved when the driver allowed us to board without paying. We couldn't believe we were finally getting closer to finding our way to America! Unfortunately, when we arrived in Austria's large capital city, it was New Year's Eve, and most businesses were closed. We had no money and no idea where to go. Once again I was grateful that I knew German. I spoke to one of the people joyfully celebrating the coming of the New Year, and she suggested that the nearby jail might allow us to spend the night—and that's exactly where we headed. The workers at the jail kindly gave us permission to stay. The boys remained with me in a cell in the women's section, and Ernő slept with the men in another part of the jail. It was an unexpected turn of events, but we had no other options. We kept reassuring the boys not to worry because we had done nothing wrong and would be leaving in the morning. It's hard to believe that we actually spent that night in jail! At least the boys had their toy buses for entertainment.

The next morning our goal was to find the United States Embassy. Someone gave me directions, warning that it would be a long, long walk. We had no car, of course, and still had no place to stay unless we wanted to return to the jail. When I saw a friendly looking woman leaving a factory, I approached her and explained that we had just arrived from Hungary, asking if she had any idea where we could stay. When I shared the story of spending the previous night in a jail cell, she smiled and said, "I live in a community up the hill, and there's an older couple who may have room for you." We followed the woman onto a bus and then trailed behind her as she walked briskly up the hill. She then introduced us to our very gracious hosts who enthusiastically welcomed us into their home. They had an extra bed and a sofa, and that's where we slept.

The kind couple, knowing that traveling to downtown Vienna and back would take many hours, suggested that we leave the boys with them when we went to the embassy. I was relieved to have somewhere safe for our sons to stay. It wasn't easy for István and György to be cared for by people speaking a foreign language, but they enjoyed playing with the other children who were on school holiday, and they quickly learned German. Everyone told us the boys were well-behaved, and soon there were good-natured arguments about who would look after them each day. We had no need to worry because our sons were having a great time frolicking in the snow, then drinking hot chocolate and eating cake as they warmed up in front of a roaring fire. And, of course, they were surrounded by love from the local families who invited us into their homes for meals and showered the boys with their favorite foods. István and György have wonderful memories of the weeks they spent being treated like celebrities in that special place.

Although we arrived early each morning, the lines at the United States Embassy seemed endless. We waited in the bitter cold day after day until we finally had a chance to talk to someone about requesting asylum. They asked if we had relatives in the United States who could sign an affidavit indicating willingness to support us if necessary. My mom's youngest brother, József, and his wife had settled in New York with their two children before World War II, so we provided their contact information. After the letter was sent, we waited for a response, clinging to the hope that the Americans would welcome us. During those anxious days, we had the good fortune of remaining in the same house, surrounded by the many people who had helped us with open hearts.

You can probably understand why it felt so wonderful to find respite and welcome in that special community. My sons were happy and well cared for, and that allowed me to finally relax. During our escape and the weeks of planning before we left, I had become the leader in the family, feeling the immense responsibility of keeping us safe. All of my energy was focused on figuring out what I needed to do next. And when we arrived in Austria, I once again needed to take the lead because I spoke German.

Even though we were not sure what our future held, I felt tremendous gratitude to everyone who had helped us along the way. When I look back, our plan could have gone wrong in so many ways. I realized that we might not have survived without the assistance of so many kind Austrians: the Red Cross workers who compassionately cared for four frozen refugees; the relief workers at the elementary school; the jail staff who gave us food and shelter; and the kind woman who led us to her welcoming community. And, of course, the wonderful couple and their neighbors who treated us as welcomed guests. As an immigrant and refugee, I can tell you that kindness such as this fills a person's heart.

35

A Few More Bumps Along the Way

Early February 1957

W e finally received the wonderful news that my uncle József had returned the necessary paperwork and we had permission to come to the United States. We would first move to a refugee camp near Salzburg and remain there until it was time to leave Europe and begin our lives in America. After saying emotional goodbyes to all of our new friends, we left for the train station, accompanied by the special couple who hosted us. That wonderful couple—always smiling and full of love—were like grandparents to my sons. We tearfully bid them farewell, sad to be leaving but ready to continue our journey. We disembarked at the refugee camp where we would remain until it was time for us to take another train through Germany and then sail from the port city of Bremerhaven across the Atlantic to New York.

Ernő was still getting over his surprise that we had managed to escape and that everything was working out for us. We were both filled with hope at the thought of finally leaving Europe, understanding that this was a major turning point in our lives and appreciating the opportunity to start over. Although we were already missing my father and Irén, neither Ernő nor I were mourning the prospect of leaving our homeland. Our reasons for leaving were painfully clear. It wasn't a regular time or a normal situation. It was after the Holocaust, after years of Communist rule, and after a revolution where the Soviets unleashed all of their military power to stop the thousands of Hungarians fighting for freedom. Living in a country where we constantly feared the Soviets and hidden Nazis, I often wondered, *If we're prevented from living with freedom, are we truly alive?* I hoped that leaving Europe would finally allow us to escape the never-ending parade of leaders and soldiers who controlled people with no concern for the human consequences of their actions.

I learned a lot during the Holocaust, including the importance of basic human rights. As I witnessed the Soviets abusing their power, I knew where that could lead. I understood what it meant to lose freedom and how it felt to have power held over me. And I knew it wasn't the life I wanted for myself or for our sons. Unfortunately, those who abuse power are often successful in generating fear, so Ernő and I had remained silent—for the simple reason that we were afraid. The terror the Soviets created was a powerful method of control, just as instilling fear had worked for the Nazis. Ernő and I were ready to close the many doors of our past and to escape the fear. I told Ernő that my biggest hope was that we would have a life where no one would threaten our freedom or our dignity. Surrounded by so many kind people during our time in Austria, I had breathed a sigh of relief, believing that the worst was behind us.

I'm sorry to say that during our final days in Europe, we were not yet free of anti-Semitism and hate. Soon after we arrived at the

A Few More Bumps Along the Way

refugee camp, another Jewish refugee from Hungary quietly warned us to be careful because some of the Hungarian refugees and some of the workers seemed like Nazis. She cautioned us, "Don't look left or right. Just keep your head down and keep on walking." We soon realized there was good reason for the warning, as hurtful comments about Jews were hurled our way. We were faced with a double dose of hatred against us, first because we were Hungarian and then because we were Jewish. We were asked, "What are you doing here? You're Hungarian; why don't you go back where you came from? You're Jewish; you don't belong here!" I asked myself, *This is going on again? I escaped Hungary for this?* Although there were many things I wanted to say to the people who were being so cruel, I knew it was best to stay silent.

We had been thrilled to arrive safely in Austria and to be on our way to America, but then this! It was unfortunate, but at least we had a place to sleep and a little bit of food. It was hard to hear the cruel things they were saying about Jews, especially because my little boys, only seven and nine years old, were also hearing those terrible words. It hurt me deeply to see our young sons come face to face with the ugliness of hate. But we had no choice since we had been assigned to wait in the camp. I tried to focus on the many kind people in Austria who had been willing to do whatever they could to help us. You can imagine how relieved we felt when the ship arrived and it was time to leave the camp. We were ready to put European anti-Semitism behind us and begin our new life in America.

36

Sailing to Freedom

Early February 1957

On February 5, 1957, Ernő, István, György, and I boarded the *General Nelson M. Walker*, a U.S. naval transport ship, and began our four-thousand-mile voyage across the Atlantic Ocean. Surrounded by other Hungarian refugees, we sailed past Great Britain's White Cliffs of Dover and then into the tumultuous Atlantic Ocean. I was finally heading toward the land I had dreamed of—the United States of America. Like the day we escaped from Hungary, I was looking forward, and didn't once look back.

We had a lot to adjust to on the ship, and the U.S. crew members did whatever they could to help us feel comfortable. Although I felt safe and protected by the sailors, crossing the Atlantic Ocean in February was a challenge. It was a very rough journey with a lot of movement. We sometimes felt totally weightless before feeling the full force of gravity abruptly pull us to the floor. Before long, many people were seasick, spending hours in their sleeping quarters on bunk beds that were stacked five people high. One day György greet-ed me by proudly announcing, "István is sick and Dad is sick, but I'm not!" But that didn't last long. With so many people ill, the cooks were happy to hand out some of their extra food, and one of the cooks kindly gave György a fresh orange. Unfortunately, my poor son, who had never before eaten an orange, had no idea he shouldn't eat the rind. The next thing I knew, György was holding his stomach and announcing he was feeling terrible. I later learned he had eaten the entire orange, peel and all. It was such an unpleasant experience that it took György twenty years to eat another orange!

Although Ernő and the boys were sick for days, I was fortunate to have a strong stomach. We hadn't had much food in the refugee camp, so meals were important to me, and I went to the cafeteria alone. The lurching of the ship forced us to hold tightly to our trays. I remember being teased one day when I put down my tray so I could step over the bench to sit down. Not speaking any English but wanting to safeguard my meal after it began sliding down the table, I yelled loudly in Hungarian, "That lunch is mine!" The people around me chuckled and reassured me that no one was going to take it away from me.

Once István and György began feeling better, they began to ex-plore the ship. To help settle his stomach, István spent as much time on the deck as possible, trying to keep his eyes on the horizon. One morning he was walking around the deck, and turning the corner, he bumped into a very large African American sailor. István, who had never seen anyone of African ancestry, looked up at this tall, muscu-lar man with his dark skin and dark eyes, screamed loudly, and ran into my arms. Of course, he had no reason to be afraid, but it was a new experience for him. We were accustomed to Hungary where al-most everyone was of European ancestry. We had a lot to learn about racial diversity in the United States.

The last few days on the ship were the best. We were all healthy and able to spend time together as a family, celebrating the fact that we would soon reach America. When our ship was finally approaching land, we waited with anticipation as we entered New York Harbor. Although our capital city of Budapest was beautiful, it was nothing like New York City. We had never seen so many buildings touching the sky. And because we were not accustomed to seeing cars, the shoreline looked like it was covered with tiny bugs running in all directions. Back in Budapest, cars were a rarity and had not yet replaced streetcars and horse-drawn carriages as the most common mode of transportation. As we sailed into the harbor, someone yelled "Look!" and everyone ran to one side of the ship. It's lucky that the ship didn't tip over with all of us charging in the same direction. And then we saw that beautiful landmark we had heard so much about—the Statue of Liberty. There she was, welcoming us as she had welcomed thousands of immigrants over the years. We were thrilled to finally arrive in the country we had dreamed of, a country that promised us freedom.

I joked with Ernő that I should write a thank-you note to the Nazis and the Soviets because it was their behavior that gave me—a quiet, easy-going schoolteacher—the strength to escape. I added that maybe I should also thank the Soviets for sending us back during our first escape attempt because that made me even more determined to leave. I teased that my note would say, "Thank you so much. You made me strong. You didn't stop me, and now my family and I are ready to start our new life in America."

Part IV

1957–2019

37

Land of the Free

February 14, 1957

E rnő, István, György, and I emerged from the naval transport ship filled with energy, eager to explore the country that was to become our home. I found it almost impossible to believe we had reached the United States of America—finally free of both Nazism and communism. Although tired from our long ocean journey, I was exhilarated as I stepped into my dream of living in America.

When the boat landed, we had no idea what to expect. We looked out at the people waiting on the dock, looking for Uncle József amidst the crowd of strangers. An official announced the army would transport all Hungarian refugees to Camp Kilmer in New Jersey where we would complete our immigration processing. Peering out the window of the bus, we were once again astonished to see roads filled with cars. We could tell that life in America was going to be quite an adventure!

Although Camp Kilmer was a bit drab, with the austerity you might expect from an army facility, it was far different from the refugee camp in Germany. Everything was clean, there was plenty of food, and, most importantly, everyone treated us with respect. The U.S military staff welcomed us and made sure we were comfortable as they worked tirelessly to match hundreds of refugees with cities welcoming immigrants. Some of the people assisting us spoke a little Hungarian, which was helpful because we didn't know a word of English. István and György felt so comfortable in the camp that one day they walked to the army office, asking for someone who spoke Hungarian. István took the lead, explaining, "We're here with our mom and dad. Our dad is a math teacher and is very smart. Do you have a job for him?" You can imagine the soldier's reaction hearing two young children so sincerely seeking work for their father.

While waiting at the camp, we were able to visit with Uncle József, his wife, Helen, and their two young sons in their apartment in New York City. I hadn't seen them for years, and it was wonderful to be with family. Uncle József had a surprise for me. His eyes brimmed with tears as he handed me a delicate pair of earrings—miniature flowers with opal petals and intricate gold stems—that had belonged to my mother. Uncle József explained that during his last visit to Hungary just before World War II, my grandmother had urged my mom to give him the heirloom for safekeeping. I tearfully thanked Uncle József for safeguarding the earrings—a precious gift connected to both my mother and grandmother. With the exception of the family photos my father retrieved from the rubble of our bombed-out home, those earrings are the only tangible link that I have to my mom.

We soon learned that city life in America was very different from Hungary. New York City seemed to have people everywhere. We were spellbound watching the traffic moving in all directions, often gasping in amazement as cars sped through traffic lights that had already turned yellow or red. I don't know how many times I heard Ernő exclaim, "Did you see that? Didn't they see the light? Someone could be killed! We need to get out of here!" I wasn't surprised that when we discussed where we would settle, Ernő announced that he wasn't interested in living in an extremely large city. Besides that, neither of us wanted to burden Uncle József by moving in with him.

When the relocation workers asked where we wanted to reside, Ernő and I told them we were looking for a smaller city that had a good college for our sons, as well as a Hungarian Jewish population. At the time, we didn't know that in America, children often attend college far from home. The workers talked among themselves and then mentioned two possibilities: St. Louis, Missouri, or Cincinnati, Ohio. Ernő and I knew nothing about either city, but István, who was listening intently, proudly shared that he had heard about St. Louis when his class studied the Mississippi River. So, our decision was made, and we were soon on a train heading to St. Louis, eager to begin our new life.

38

So Much to Learn

1957

When we arrived in St. Louis, we were grateful for the assistance and warm welcome we received from the Hebrew Immigration Aid Society (HIAS) and the local Jewish community. They arranged for us to stay in a hotel in downtown St. Louis. It was certainly not the Hilton, so we were delighted when a Jewish factory owner, who had read about our arrival, generously offered us an apartment and helped us with necessities until we were able to pay our own way. Using German or German Yiddish, I was able to communicate with European immigrants who had resettled after fleeing the Nazis, and these new friends assisted us in learning about American culture. Neither Ernő nor I were accustomed to relying on other people, but we appreciated everyone's kindness and the opportunity to focus on becoming independent. Learning English became an immediate priority because even simple tasks like shopping or traveling on the bus can be extremely difficult if you don't speak or read the language where you're living.

Fortunately, Ernő was soon employed as a cantor at our syna-gogue—a job that didn't require English because our prayers are sung in Hebrew. This was another big change for our family. In Hungary, our sons barely knew they were Jewish, and suddenly Judaism be-came a big part of our lives. Our family was expected to follow kosher traditions, a requirement associated with Ernő's position as cantor, and we accompanied Ernő to the synagogue every Friday night and Saturday morning. For about a month, István and György attended the Epstein Hebrew Academy where half of the classes were taught in Hebrew. However, we soon decided it was best for them to attend public school where they could spend the entire day learning in English rather than trying to learn two new languages at once.

Ernő and I almost immediately found full-time employment as factory workers. The factory owner who was helping us hired Ernő as a manual laborer with the task of upholstering bar stools, and I started a job in another factory—in a place many would call a "sweat-shop"—where we worked hour after hour in an incredibly hot room sewing military hats. After receiving instructions, pantomimed be-cause I didn't understand English, I sat before a sewing machine, counting the minutes until I could return home. My employer hired many immigrants, perhaps because we were hard workers who sti-fled any complaints because we wanted to keep our jobs.

Although it was a challenge to go from careers we enjoyed to fac-tory labor, Ernő and I were delighted to receive a paycheck and proud to pay for food and rent. Those first years were especially difficult for Ernő, but he never complained. For me, it was a gift that he seemed to understand our circumstances were temporary and that we could become teachers again once we learned English and returned to col-lege. We also had the goal of learning about American history and government so we could apply for citizenship, confident that if we worked hard, our dream of becoming U.S. citizens would come true.

Ernő and I celebrated when we both managed to find new, more appealing jobs. After hearing that the owners of a costume jewelry store—German Jews who had escaped the Nazis—were looking for an employee who could speak and write German, I applied. You can imagine my delight when they hired me and I was able leave that hot, humid factory. One year in that sweatshop was quite enough for me! Although my new job was not easy, it was a big improvement. I took each customer's order, written in German by the German-speaking owner, and then climbed up a tall ladder to retrieve each inventory item requested. And Ernő was relieved to leave his exhausting upholstery work when his employer discovered he was an excellent mathematician and offered him a position in the accounting department. Ernő was delighted at the change, especially because he had the opportunity to use his math skills. When working in the office, Ernő decided to change his name to Earnest, the English translation of his name. My dear husband was clear about the spelling he wanted to use, insisting that his name match the spelling on the paychecks he was writing to other workers. Even after I explained that Ernest Hemingway spelled his name differently, he was very definite that he wanted to use the spelling "Earnest," so I said no more about it.

When we visited my uncle József in New York City soon after we arrived, he realized we had no money, so he gave us $100 to help us get started, assuring us we didn't need to reimburse him. Nevertheless, Earnest had a different idea. Although he appreciated the gift, Earnest was determined to repay every penny. This was the first time in his life that Earnest owed money, and he didn't like the feeling. So what did he do? After receiving his very first paycheck, Earnest wired $100 to József, determined to pay his debt without delay.

When we first arrived in America, Earnest and I didn't have the time or the strength to focus on anything other than finding a job and getting through each day, but within a year, we were managing on our own. We were careful with our money, watching every penny as if it were our last, and doing our best not to waste anything or throw away any items that might be useful in the future. My sons say Earnest and I treated whatever we had as if it was a treasure. When we saved a bit of money, someone told us we should deposit it in a bank—a new concept for us because we had never before had an opportunity to save money. When the man completing the paperwork for our account asked us if we had any loans or owed any money, Earnest's face flushed at what he perceived to be an insult, and he indignantly responded, "Me? Owe money? Never in my life have I owed one penny that I didn't pay back! If I buy something, I pay for it! If I don't have the money to pay for something, then I don't get it!" That was my dear husband making his position very clear to the bewildered bank employee. Throughout his life, Earnest continued to feel strongly about not borrowing money; even when we needed to buy a car or were ready to buy a house, we waited until we were able to pay cash.

Although those first years were challenging, I woke up every morning feeling grateful that we were free and safe from the Nazis and the Soviets. That was something to celebrate! I tried to keep that feeling alive, especially when we were feeling exhausted. We knew what we needed to accomplish if we wanted to succeed and make our dream of becoming citizens a reality.

39

A New Way of Life

1957–1958

Earnest and I, eager to learn the language of our new country, immediately enrolled in the intensive English classes offered to immigrants at our local community college. Although we studied hard, hoping to learn quickly, we soon discovered English is not an easy language. Even now, after sixty years in the United States, no one can miss my strong Hungarian accent. Although Earnest and I spoke to each other in Hungarian, we asked the boys to use English at home so we could learn as much as possible. They enjoyed practicing with us, and proudly corrected our mistakes.

In my quest to broaden my English vocabulary, I went to the public library and borrowed books by Mark Twain, confident that my old friends Tom Sawyer and Huck Finn would help me learn English. I knew the plots and the characters from reading about their adventures in Hungarian, so I focused on learning the words in English. I also reread the book *The Forty Days of Musa Dagh* for the first time since the Holocaust, this time intensely identifying with the pain and inhumanity of the forty-day Armenian genocide.

English is a complicated language, and the idioms sometimes gave me trouble. When some new friends took us to a restaurant and I was unable to eat everything on my plate, the waiter noticed my worried expression and asked, "Ma'am, is something wrong?" When I explained, "I don't want to waste the food, but it's too much for me to finish," the young man reassured me, "Don't worry. I'll give you a doggie bag." Having never heard that idiom, I protested, "But I don't have a dog!" That poor man did his best to keep a straight face, but when he went into the kitchen, I could hear laughter as he told his coworkers what I had said. When our friends explained, I had to smile, understanding completely why the waiter was trying so hard not to laugh.

Earnest and I did all we could to ensure that István and György were adjusting to our new life. We encouraged them to embrace being American, and they soon decided it would be easier to use the English versions of their names—so István became Steve and György became George. In March 1957, Steve entered the fourth grade and George entered the second grade, their first formal education since the previous October when the Hungarian Revolution caused schools to close. They both worked hard to keep up with their peers using their limited English skills. Steve was fortunate to have a classmate born in Hungary who helped translate during his first few weeks of school. Steve made friends easily, in part because his experience kicking soccer balls in Hungary resulted in an ability to propel the ball farther than anyone else in his grade. Although Steve and George learned English quickly, it was sometimes challenging to be different from their peers. Most of the children were helpful, although Steve remembers a sixth-grade classmate mocking his slight accent. At Steve's fiftieth high school reunion, that same boy, now a grown man, apologized for being unkind, and of course, Steve accepted the unexpected apology.

When the school year ended, someone in our congregation arranged for Steve and George to spend three weeks at a Jewish summer camp. As the group of excited children eagerly left for camp, the other mothers seemed cheerful, looking forward to weeks of freedom. In contrast, instead of smiling, I was crying, unable to hide my distress at the thought of my young sons being away for so long. My heart felt like it would burst with sadness. Although three weeks away seemed like forever, when the boys returned home and excitedly recounted their adventures using their much-improved English, Earnest and I realized it had been a good decision to allow them to go.

I discovered I had a lot to learn about American customs. When someone explained to me that in St. Louis it was customary to take off your shoes when entering someone's house, I remember my surprise, asking, "What else do we need to take off here in America?" Sometimes our European customs collided with American customs, but having children helped teach me it was important to be flexible. Earnest always had very clear ideas of what was acceptable and what was not, and he was slow to accept many of the new customs. I didn't want to hold our boys back in adjusting to our new country, so I told Earnest, "We're in America, and we need to learn American ways." Yet it wasn't always easy, even for me. Steve came home from school one day, excited because a friend had invited him to dinner. Despite his enthusiasm, I protested, "No way! You need to eat your meals with us." Earnest and I couldn't imagine our child going to a friend's house to eat when we had food for him at home. Other immigrants encouraged us to allow our sons to spend time with their peers, so we began to reluctantly agree. One custom we never gave up, however, was Hungarian cooking. The boys always looked forward to a good Hungarian meal, especially chicken paprikash with Hungarian noodles or a potato, sausage, and egg casserole served with a cucumber salad. And, of course, we all enjoyed the dessert tradition of Hungarian pastry filled with jam, cheese, nuts, or chocolate.

In Hungary, when we needed new clothes, we bought material and stitched the clothes ourselves. I was surprised when people told me that in America you look for a sale and buy your clothes in a store, and if the clothing doesn't fit, the store allows you to return it. In Europe, we had nothing like that! One day I realized that some shorts I had bought for George were too small, so I stood in the long line at the Sears store, holding the shorts and the receipt. When it was my turn to approach the counter, I explained, "I am from Hungary, and I have never returned clothing before because we make our clothes by hand. I had never heard of bringing back clothes if you don't like them, but my friends told me I could. It seems unbelievable that I'm allowed to return these shorts that don't fit my son, but I brought the receipt because my friend told me I needed to show my receipt." The poor man at the counter, aware of the long line behind me, didn't want to hear any further explanation, so he grabbed the shorts and the receipt and almost shouted, "Ma'am, you want to return these shorts? Then give them to me!" As he refunded my money, I thought, *If my mom or grandma heard this story about returning clothing that doesn't fit, they would never believe it!* Despite my desire to comment further, I knew I had better not tell the man at the counter what I was thinking because I had probably already given him too much information.

I was happy to discover that the Noémi Ban who arrived from Europe was the same Noémi Ban starting life over in America. I wanted to be independent, and we soon learned that in America being independent means knowing how to drive a car. We never had a car in Hungary—that was only for the very rich people and then for the Communists—so neither Earnest nor I knew how to drive. We saved money to buy a car, and once Earnest began to drive, I was determined to learn, too. Earnest was forty-five when he first started driving, and I was thirty-five. When Earnest heard I wanted him to teach me, he was incredulous, asking, "You want to learn to drive? You must be kidding!" I answered, "I am completely serious. I not only *want* to learn to drive, I *will* learn to drive. There's a difference." Seeing that I was determined, Earnest found a big parking lot and began teaching me how to maneuver the car. It was a humorous scene with Earnest, a brand-new driver himself, telling me, "You're going too slow! You're going too fast!" with our sons laughing in the back seat. It wasn't easy, but I soon became an independent woman who could drive if I wanted to.

Earnest and I, eager to continue our teaching careers, began taking the college classes required for our Missouri teaching certificates. We worked during the day and took most of our college courses at night.

Earnest was able to finish in one year because mathematical equations are mathematical equations, and he was delighted when the principal at Bayless High School hired him. Earnest, who dressed for work in a long-sleeved shirt and tie even in hot and humid weather, was known for his high expectations and his perseverance in teaching challenging concepts. He was usually patient but became frustrated when students didn't seem to care about learning, reminding them how fortunate they were to study in a free society. Mathematics came easily to Earnest, so he had a hard time understanding why a hard-working student might struggle to understand algebra or calculus. One such student recalled coming to his classroom three afternoons each week for extra help, sometimes fighting tears at the difficulty she was having with algebra despite her good grades in her other courses. Although Earnest had a hard time comprehending why she didn't understand math concepts, he really wanted her to succeed. One afternoon, in his typical straightforward manner and with his strong Hungarian accent, he bluntly stated, "I have never seen anyone try so hard but perform so poorly." Fortunately, the student, understanding that Earnest would never deliberately be cruel, responded with laughter rather than tears.

It took me longer to return to the classroom because my major required three years of coursework—a wonderful opportunity to improve my English and learn about everything American. I was eager to study a noncommunist version of history, and to learn more about World War II. With every part of my being, I wanted to comprehend how it was possible for the Nazis to murder millions of innocent people, and why the Western world didn't do more to stop Hitler. I wanted to understand why there was American resistance to allowing European Jews who were fleeing the Nazis to come to the United States, especially once leaders knew about Hitler's campaign of genocide. Although I listened carefully in class and read every book I could find on the topic, I never mentioned I was a Holocaust survivor with firsthand knowledge of what we were studying.

I finally began to share my experiences as a prisoner when an English professor assigned us the task of writing personal stories about life-changing events. His assignments encouraged me to share details of the experience that most profoundly changed my life—the Holocaust. I had much I wanted to say, but I struggled with the essays, finding it difficult to express myself with my limited English. After I finished each paper, I asked my sons to check my spelling and grammar. They were proud when I asked for their assistance, and it also proved to be an opportunity for them to learn about my life as a Nazi prisoner. Until then, they had no knowledge of the Holocaust.

As they were reading, they would ask, "Mom, did this happen to you?" When they begged me to tell them more, I reluctantly answered. Still, I tried not to say too much. I didn't want to traumatize my sons by sharing more than they could handle. I understood the importance of being honest and open with children, but I also wanted to make sure that our sons never felt different from other children because their parents were Holocaust survivors. I never wanted our experiences to be a burden for them.

The professor was very interested in what I wrote, telling me he stayed up late reading every word. He said the stories were important and that people should know what happened. While taking that class, I realized I was feeling free. I was free to write. I was free to share my experiences. When I read my essays to my classmates, they asked questions and seemed to care. Nevertheless, I did not share my story again for several decades.

I was delighted when I finally completed my college classes, received my teacher certification, and began working as a long-term substitute in a sixth-grade classroom. At the end of the year, the district offered me a position teaching high school, but instead of immediately accepting, I asked the elementary principal if it would be possible for me to continue teaching sixth grade. He agreed, and I had the privilege of teaching sixth graders at Oakdale Elementary School for sixteen years. Sixth grade is a wonderful age because students are interested in new experiences and want to know everything. I loved every minute of those wonderful years.

I encouraged my students to reach out to books because I firmly believe that books can help people make connections and gather ideas for dealing with difficult situations. I know that books have always helped me. I was surprised that our sixth graders weren't reading American classics, so I brought stories by authors such as Mark Twain and Pearl Buck into the classroom. I didn't know much about Christmas in America, but my class always celebrated with freshly baked cookies and gift exchanges. When I brought in the book *A Christmas Carol* by Charles Dickens, the students enjoyed reading the story and then acting out their favorite scenes.

I spoke with my students about prejudice and discrimination and encouraged discussions of topics such as how U.S. families of Japanese descent must have felt when forced into internment camps during World War II. We talked about the killing and displacement of Indigenous people that occurred when European settlers arrived in America and took over their land. When I taught about slavery, we discussed how it would feel to be kidnapped and transported to a strange place in the cargo hold of a ship or to be separated from family members and forced to work as a slave. We also spoke about children who were born into slavery and never had a chance to experience freedom. I wanted my students to be able to think critically about history and about world events.

When I taught about the history or geography of Europe, I told my students a bit about my life after the war and our escape into Austria. I asked them to think about the meaning of freedom and to imagine a life without freedom. My students listened carefully and always wanted to hear more. Yet I never told them I was a Nazi prisoner or that I was Jewish. Although I was no longer wearing the yellow star, the fear and humiliation from those difficult years still dwelled deep inside me.

I introduced my sixth graders to the idea of a brown bag classroom lunch, and many of my students joined me for lunch nearly every day, eager to work on special activities like learning to crochet. Even the boys enjoyed crocheting! I not only loved the extra time with my students, but I also enjoyed getting to know them in a more informal setting. I found that learning about their interests and experiences allowed me to more effectively teach each child. I hoped my students would know that if something was bothering them, they could come to me and I would listen with love and understanding. Although my students were unaware of my life story, I was often able to convince a distressed student that no matter what happened, sadness doesn't go on forever and that there is always hope.

I wanted my students to understand their value as human beings, so I was careful never to talk down to them, always remembering how I felt when the Nazis, the Soviets, and anti-Semitic Europeans treated me with disrespect. I tried to keep a child's self-image in mind, even when a student's behavior required correction. When I was teaching students who struggled with learning, I concentrated on helping them regain their self-respect and belief in their ability to improve.

After my sixteenth year in that sixth-grade classroom, Earnest retired. Even though I was only in my early sixties, I followed him into retirement so we could proceed with our plan to move to Bellingham, Washington, to live close to our son Steve, our daughter-in-law, Jan, and our three grandchildren, Rachel, Julia, and Miriam. Once I announced I was retiring, Earnest was reluctant to show up at my school, worried that the parents of the upcoming sixth graders might not forgive him for taking me away. It was not easy to leave the sixth grade after so many years, and I have never forgotten all of my wonderful students. I loved each one of them with all my heart.

40

Connecting with the Past

About fifteen years after our escape, Earnest and I were finally able to afford a trip to Hungary—the only time I was able to visit my father before he died in 1982 at eighty-six years of age. When we arrived in America, Earnest and I hoped that my father and Irén would eventually join us. However, the Communist government continued in Hungary until 1989, so Soviet control was still in effect when my father died. Besides that, my father felt it would be too difficult to start a new life, reminding us, "An old tree cannot be replanted." We kept in touch through letters and occasional phone calls, but had only that one precious visit—a trip that was a good reminder of why we were so happy to escape.

Earnest and I were nervous as the plane touched down in Hungary. Although we both had U.S. passports, we were concerned what the Communists might do if they discovered we had escaped in 1956. It did not go well. I did my best to act unconcerned when the Communist officials directed us to an interrogation room, but my mouth was so dry I could barely speak. After lecturing us about escaping, they presented us with what seemed like a thousand questions, repeatedly asking, "Why would you want to go to America instead of staying in Hungary?" After we endured their speeches and questions, they released us. As we were going through the interrogation, I thought to myself, *This is exactly why we wanted to leave.* Of course, I didn't say a word.

When we first retired and moved to Bellingham, Earnest and I finally had the opportunity for more travel. One of our first priorities was visiting our younger son, George, an international pharmaceutical director based on the East Coast, and his two children—our granddaughter, Karen, and our only grandson, Jason. It was wonderful to see them, and we enjoyed talking about George's foreign travels and our grandchildren's lives. We also began to plan their next visit to Bellingham, looking forward to having both of our sons and all of our grandchildren together. It's not easy when loved ones live so far away.

We then decided to combine a trip to Israel with travel to Germany and Hungary. While exploring Israel—a beautiful country with an amazing history—I had the pleasure of finally meeting Earnest's sister who had settled in Israel, the only one of his six sisters to survive the Holocaust. She was delighted to see Earnest after so many years. And what an experience it was to see Hebrew everywhere we went! Although I knew how to read Hebrew prayers, I was unable to understand the day-to-day Hebrew I saw everywhere, and it took a while to become accustomed to seeing delivery vehicles and garbage trucks with Hebrew words on them. Earnest had difficulty getting around in Israel, and I assumed the colloquial Hebrew was confusing him, too. Unfortunately, we later learned his difficulties were something else entirely.

After exploring Israel, Earnest and I traveled to Germany to visit Allendorf, where I attended a reunion of survivors of the Münchmühle camp, including many of the one thousand Hungarian women who had traveled with me from Auschwitz-Birkenau. The love we received from the community and their sincere attempt to make amends for the Nazi era brought many of us to tears.

We then traveled to Hungary to visit Irén and to spend time with Earnest's brother, Sándor, and his sons. It was wonderful to see the family, but it was also sad because it was my first visit since my father had passed away almost a decade earlier. Irén generously gave me the family photos my father had treasured, including a tiny portrait my mother sent to him when he was imprisoned in Siberia during World War I. When my father first found some of our family photos in the rubble where our house had stood, he had no idea how precious those mementos would become. He kept them close to him for his entire life, and they are now among my most prized possessions, hanging on a memorial wall in my home so I am able to look at them every day. Those pictures tell a lot. They show a loving family. They show who we were before the war, and before the killing.

Irén also gave me another beautiful gift during that visit—the journal my father wrote in as he was searching for us after his escape from Nazi captivity. I learned a lot about my father when I painstakingly translated his journal, transcribing every word into English. I cried as I read the words my father wrote at such a heartbreaking time in his life—tears of sadness over the loss of the loved ones who had been stolen from our lives, but also tears of joy because I realized that the Nazis did not rob us of our love, our memories, or our hope. Although I read the diary decades after my father had poured out his heart, I could feel the pain and suffering he experienced during those heart-wrenching days after he returned to find a bombed house and no evidence that we were alive. As I read what my father had written day after day, I knew he was wise not to keep his pain locked inside. Even though he never spoke to me about his deepest feelings, I could see that expressing his pain in writing had helped him survive and eventually move on with his life. I'm not sure what would have happened if he had kept such tremendous pain bottled inside. My father had a beautiful way of writing, and his journal remains a heartbreaking testament to his feelings during those dark days and a lasting tribute to the loved ones who never returned.

Irén also shared a memoir my father wrote in Hebrew during his final years, full of memories of his first meeting with my mom and their early life together as well as the despair he felt when he realized he would never see her again. He also wrote about his imprisonment during World War I and World War II and his rediscovered happiness when he met Irén after the war. Fortunately, I was able to read the memoir when a visiting Israeli scholar was kind enough to translate my father's words from Hebrew into English.

After my father's death, I visited Irén every time I went to Europe, and we regularly talked on the phone until she passed away at the age of 101. At the end of each visit, I did my best to appear cheerful as I reassured her, "I'll see you again very soon." At the same time, I was fighting back tears, never knowing if I was saying a final farewell to the dear woman who never hesitated to love me like her very own daughter.

41

Lasting Love

During our visit to Hungary and Israel, I noticed that Earnest was having difficulty communicating in Hungarian. At times, it seemed he had not only forgotten his native language, but was also struggling with English. Although I tried to convince myself that perhaps international travel had been too much for Earnest, I began to realize it might be something much more serious. Soon, there were too many warning signs to ignore. I began to discover food in the washing machine and dirty clothes in the refrigerator. I tried not to make a big deal about what I was seeing, but I realized I needed to speak with our doctor. When I first discussed my concerns, the doctor focused on Earnest's difficulties with communicating and diagnosed aphasia. However, after more incidents of bread and milk showing up in the washing machine, he acknowledged that Earnest had dementia. When Earnest began experiencing tremors and difficulty swallowing, he added one more diagnosis: Parkinson's disease. Although I hadn't driven a car since first learning to drive years earlier in St. Louis, I applied for a Washington license and took over all the driving.

Although it isn't always easy, a crucial element of being a survivor is understanding the importance of facing and accepting the truth. At the beginning, I covered up for Earnest and minimized his symptoms. It was difficult because I had to play two roles—the wife who knew she was losing her husband and the woman who wanted to reassure herself and others that everything was fine. Then one day, I looked in the mirror, telling myself, *Okay. Let's be honest. Earnest is sick, and every day he is worse. You can't cover for him anymore.* That was an important turning point. Instead of losing valuable time hiding the truth, I was finally able to use my energy to make the time we had together worthwhile.

I soon became a full-time caregiver. There were days when I was reduced to a puddle of tears as I was confronted with messes. I struggled with thoughts such as *I can't cope. I feel so lost. This is terrible.* Then I would pull myself together, reminding myself, *You need to be strong.* I would clean up the mess and recover until the next time. I began to consider why Earnest's accidents bothered me so much and remembered the latrines in Auschwitz. When we were sitting on the latrine, often feeling so ill we could barely move, the kapos had no sympathy as they yelled for us to line up to be counted, often picking us up by our ears or the rags we were wearing. Making this connection, I better understood my reactions and reminded myself that those horrors were in the past: *You can't equate it with what is happening here with your husband. You love him.* After that, cleaning up was never a pleasure, but at least my extreme distress had vanished.

As I was losing my dear husband to dementia, I sometimes felt down, but darkness never overtook me. Even in Auschwitz, I was able to hold on to some hope. Like everyone, I have days when I feel blue, but it doesn't last. When I was caring for Earnest, if I began to feel somewhat hopeless, I did my best to get out of it by identifying exactly what was bothering me, stepping away from my emotions, looking at the situation objectively, and deciding how to handle it. This approach usually allowed me to return to the sunny side and walk away from the blues.

I remembered how Earnest patiently watched over me when I was recovering from the Holocaust, so I dedicated my life to caring for him with love and patience. In his quiet way, Earnest had showered me with love and devotion throughout our years together. As Earnest's dementia progressed, you can imagine how much I missed the intelligent man who had been my life partner. I was heartbroken to see his mind locked in a prison he was unable to escape.

When I took Earnest for medical checkups, the doctor always asked, "Noémi, how are you?" Although I protested, "Earnest is your patient, not me!" the doctor understood the challenges of caregiving and losing someone to dementia. It wasn't safe to leave Earnest alone, so I stayed home or took him with me everywhere I went. When people asked me, "Noémi, when will you start looking for a nursing home for Earnest?" I always answered, "What do you mean? If someone you love has problems, you don't ship them away. He isn't going anywhere! He's staying here with me!" I'm not criticizing people who need to move a family member who requires assistance. Many people have no other choice, and I understand. I was lucky that I was ten years younger than Earnest and able to care for him in our own home.

My family encouraged me to find a way to spend some time alone, even if it was only for a few hours each week. When I finally admitted that I was feeling like a prisoner in my own house because Earnest was so dependent on me, we hired Patty, a loving professional caregiver, to stay with Earnest for two hours each week while I left to take a piano lesson. Although I hadn't played for decades, it came back quickly and rekindled my childhood delight at playing the piano.

As Earnest's needs increased beyond what Patty could provide, we hired Harriet, another compassionate caregiver. Although Earnest was initially skeptical about having two strangers helping with his personal care, he grew comfortable with both Patty and Harriet, and they soon became like family. Earnest showed he cared for Patty by stepping close and rearranging her collar or sleeves, whereas he enjoyed holding Harriet's hand and rhythmically twisting her wedding ring. Still, whenever I returned home, a huge smile lit up his face and his blue eyes sparkled with absolute happiness, reminding me how much he loved and needed me.

Even with Patty and Harriet's help, Earnest and I continued to spend a lot of time together. Although Earnest was no longer able to read, I knew how much he loved books, so I often handed him a book and he entertained himself turning the pages. When Earnest started pacing, I discovered that going out for a walk or giving him some yarn to wind into a ball helped him relax. Although Earnest could no longer communicate with me, I spoke to him constantly as we went through his daily routine. I wanted to make both of our lives easier.

Understanding the importance of family support, my son Steve and his wife, Jan, encouraged me to sell our house and to build a new one on the vacant lot adjoining their home. Earnest enjoyed watching the progress on the construction, and when we moved in, he loved watching the birds soaring through the air and the boats cruising in the coastal waterway below us. We designed the house so Earnest could live as independently as possible. Steve and Jan checked in with us regularly, and as Earnest's health declined, Jan came over every evening to help me get Earnest ready for bed, taking time to chat with me before returning home.

As the Parkinson's and dementia progressed, Earnest had difficulty chewing and was no longer able to feed himself, so I prepared soft food and spoon-fed him each meal. It took extra time to make food that Earnest could easily swallow, so when a friend suggested that perhaps Earnest could eat baby food, I bought some small jars of Earnest's favorite vegetables and fruits, excited at the prospect of no longer needing to constantly puree his meals. However, when I gave him a bite of peas, Earnest immediately spit them out of his mouth. As I sat there holding a spoon and dish of puréed vegetables with green peas all over my face, Earnest grinned at me, well aware that those puréed peas were not the Hungarian cooking he had enjoyed for years. Seeing that smile, I responded in Hungarian, "Okay. Don't worry. I'm going to cook for you." I gave away the baby food and continued to painstakingly prepare the foods that Earnest had always enjoyed.

One day while Earnest was dozing in his chair, I used the opportunity to go to the restroom. When I returned, the chair was empty. After frantically checking all the rooms and not finding Earnest anywhere, I ran down our driveway searching for him. Relief washed over me when I spotted him standing in the middle of the road at the foot of our steep hill. He was wearing socks but no shoes. He smiled at me with a look of triumph as if saying, "I made it without you!" I ran to him, linking my arm through his and doing my best to appear calm. Whenever I felt frustrated with situations like this, I kept my patience by reminding myself that Earnest was not deliberately being difficult. Instead, his behavior came from something he was unable to control—his dementia. Patty, Harriet, and I decided we needed a plan to prevent Earnest from leaving without supervision, so I put a lock on the door and crocheted three lanyards so we could each carry a key. Not surprisingly, when Earnest saw our keys, he made it very clear that he wanted one, too. So I crocheted a cord for Earnest that matched ours, complete with his own key.

It wasn't an easy time. As the days passed and there were more frightening episodes, I reminded myself that all I could do was try my best to care for my dear husband, showing him every day that I loved him and would watch over him just as he had watched over me.

As Earnest became increasingly ill, our main outings were our daily walks and doctor appointments, so I looked forward to Sundays when Steve and Jan's three daughters came over to visit. Their youngest daughter, Miriam, enjoyed drawing pictures of birds for Earnest while their middle daughter, Julia, spent her time talking with him, sometimes asking me, "Why doesn't Grandpa answer us anymore?" Rachel, the oldest, sat close to her grandfather, quietly completing her homework. Those family visits were wonderful for me, and I have a feeling that Earnest felt the same way.

I began attending a dementia caregivers' support group, and eventually the leaders asked me to teach the group, sharing some of the strategies I used with Earnest. I explained our routines for showering, grooming, and dressing as well as ways to make shaving easier, laughing as I told them how I always gave Earnest kisses on both of his cheeks and on his forehead after we completed the shave. I shared the story of some close friends who watched me shave Earnest one morning and how the husband joked with his wife, saying, "I'm not shaving myself anymore. From now on, you need to shave me and shower me with kisses, too." Earnest was listening, and I saw a glint of recognition in his eyes, and perhaps even a smile. My most important message to the group was that caregivers should try to do everything with love because providing assistance with genuine compassion is as important for the person providing the care as it is for the person receiving the care. I told them how I reminded myself about the many wonderful years of love that Earnest and I had shared. Although remembering that love didn't make caregiving any less demanding, it did increase my patience and lift my spirits.

Our younger son, George, traveled from New York to visit Earnest several months before his death. Wanting to spend time with his father, George suggested, "Dad, let's go outside on the deck." Sadly, Earnest didn't want to be alone with George or be touched or hugged by someone he thought was a stranger. He kept looking at me as if asking, "Who is this guy?" That visit was a heartbreaking example of what happens during late-stage dementia.

Earnest was very ill during the last two months of his life. On the day he died, some friends were coming to visit. Although Earnest was sleeping all of the time, I carefully shaved his face, washed his hair, and kissed both of his cheeks. A few hours later, Earnest opened his eyes for the first time in days, and he looked right at me. Not long afterward, one week before we would have celebrated his eighty-second birthday and four months before our forty-ninth wedding anniversary, my dear husband died in my arms. I was almost seventy-two years old, but in those first days after losing Earnest, I felt as frightened and alone as a lost child.

Music gave me strength and emotional support in Auschwitz, during Earnest's illness, after Earnest's death, and continues to give me strength to this day. When Earnest became ill, almost five decades after the heartbreaking day when the ghetto workers carried away my beloved piano, I made the decision it was finally time to play again. Of course, I started with simple pieces of music, working my way back to the classics I had played when I was young. Reconnecting with the joy of music rekindled memories of the security I felt when surrounded by my parents' love. For me, hearing or playing music is like pushing a button—it evokes intense memories that swirl across time and touch my soul. Music fills my heart. When I sit at the piano, place my fingers on the keys, and begin playing the haunting tunes I learned a lifetime ago, I experience a deep connection with both the uplifting and the heartbreaking parts of my past. As I play each note, I can picture my mother's beautiful smile as she relaxed and enjoyed the melodies, with my father playing beside me on his violin. It's wonderful to go back to a time and place when I felt such love and security and innocence—before we had any idea of the horrors that would come.

Music also evokes the deep pain and sadness of loss—memories of our beautiful piano being carried away; my final moments with my mother, grandmother, sister, and baby brother; and holding Earnest in my arms as he took his last breath. Even now, when I play the piano each day, it's a time of deep emotion. I never know for sure which emotion it will be, so I wait and see. Whatever happens is fine with me; any emotion is beautiful because it shows that I am alive—just like a musical composition comes to life each time someone plays the notes. Music is a push that opens up my heart. Music will always be beautiful for me. After Earnest died, music brought forward wonderful memories from the almost half century that we were married, and those loving memories once more brought me to life.

42

Returning

A few months after Earnest's death, I received an invitation to attend the international reunion of Holocaust survivors scheduled to be held in Florida in February 1995, an event marking the fiftieth anniversary of the Allies' defeat of the Nazis. I mentioned the invitation to Harriet, who had kept in close touch even though she was no longer caring for Earnest, and was delighted when she decided to accompany me.

The reunion was an experience of a lifetime for both of us. I couldn't hold back my tears when a group of World War II veterans marched into the room carrying U.S. flags. I wished I could have hugged each and every one of those brave men! It was also very healing to be with other survivors, like a reunion of a special family; when I had the chance to meet with other Hungarians, there were few dry eyes as we reunited. It was amazing to discover women who suffered alongside me fifty years earlier. Overall, it was a happy occasion, although it saddened me to see some survivors become argumentative and impatient as we waited in long lines. Perhaps they had not yet been able to let go of their anger about what happened during the Holocaust.

We had the privilege of listening to a keynote address by Professor Elie Wiesel, the survivor, scholar, and Nobel Peace Prize recipient who authored almost sixty books, including his widely read memoir *Night*. Although he was about five years younger than I, Professor Wiesel and I had a lot in common since we were both among the Hungarians sent first to Auschwitz and then to a Buchenwald labor camp. Professor Wiesel gave a powerful speech about his experiences, and it felt like his words were my words. He encouraged us to share our stories with whomever would listen, allowing the listeners to become witnesses with the ability to educate others.

Another presenter, discussing the topic of Holocaust denial, again emphasized how important it is for survivors to step forward and share the details of our experiences. Unfortunately, many neo-Nazis and white supremacists have claimed that the Holocaust never occurred. Some even call it a hoax. I don't understand why these people are determined to deny the Nazi atrocities, but fortunately legitimate historians have ensured that the testimonies of both survivors and soldiers who came to our rescue are preserved. It upsets me greatly when someone says the Holocaust didn't happen. I am a peaceful person, but I feel a deep anger when I hear such a senseless and reckless statement. My question to Holocaust deniers is this: "If the Holocaust is a myth, then what happened to my mother, my grandmother, my sister, and my brother, and all of my other relatives? Where are they?" I know where they are. The Nazis murdered them in the gas chamber at Auschwitz-Birkenau and then threw their bodies into the furnaces until they became no more than ashes. How can anyone deny that cruel reality? I was a witness to the ongoing fires and clouds of ash. I wish it were different, but I have no doubt about what happened to my dear ones. Our survivors' reunion was a huge catalyst for me, setting me on a mission to counteract Holocaust denial by telling my story to whomever would listen.

Once I was home, I couldn't stop thinking about Auschwitz-Birkenau. I began imagining what it would be like to return to the site of Nazi power, but this time as a free woman. I wanted to see Auschwitz from the outside looking in, and to learn exactly what happened there. I kept envisioning myself standing in that place of horror, giving my love and respect to my dear ones. Before long, I made a decision—to return to the place that forever changed my life.

I mentioned my plan to Dr. Ray Wolpow, a professor at Western Washington University and a member of our synagogue, who had interviewed me for his doctoral dissertation. That interview was the beginning of a long friendship, a relationship that grew even stronger when Ray decided to join me on my journey to the Auschwitz-Birkenau Memorial in Poland. As a historiographer, Ray wanted to document my experience using photographs, audio recordings, and field notes. Although it wasn't part of our original plan, when we returned, Ray and I worked together to write a book, *Sharing is Healing: A Holocaust Survivor's Story*, a short memoir of my Holocaust experiences appropriate for young readers.

Before visiting Poland with Ray, I traveled alone to Budapest. I first went to see Irén, my stepmother, who still lived in the same small apartment she had shared with my father for decades, a residence permeated by the fragrance of her perfume. She still cooked in her tiny kitchen and had the same ancient bottles sitting atop an old-fashioned pull-string toilet. Irén was as talkative as ever, filling me in on her opinions about all the local gossip.

I also had a chance to visit Teca, one of the three friends who saved me in Auschwitz-Birkenau. Reuniting for the first time since the war, Teca and I clung to each other, laughing and crying as we celebrated being alive. When Teca asked if I remembered fainting in Birkenau, I told her it was a day I would never forget, assuring her I would remain forever grateful that she, her older sister, and her niece had risked their lives to save me. Teca said they still spoke of me, recalling how we supported each other while imprisoned and after liberation. Teca mentioned that she regularly met with a group of fellow survivors, always chatting about the present and the future, but never discussing the past. She teasingly told me they were all jealous of me, explaining, "We all survived, but you became an American."

When Ray arrived, I introduced him to my family and to Lili Bosch, the dear friend who helped with our escape into Austria. As we sat around a large wooden table, Ray smiled as he watched Lili and me happily chatting in Hungarian; he later told me that although he didn't understand a word we were saying, he could see how delighted we were to see each other. Although Lili confirmed to Ray that she was a prisoner in Auschwitz, the discussion quickly moved to present-day events. In Hungary, it is rare to find survivors willing to discuss their experiences with the Nazis.

When it was time for Ray and me to leave for Poland, Irén passionately argued with me about returning to Auschwitz. Irén had also been imprisoned there, but she coped by keeping her memories deep inside. Although we were very close, Irén never once spoke to me about her experiences, nor asked about mine. She simply could not understand my desire to return, asking me why I would use my time in Europe going to that terrible place. I tried to explain. "I finally have the courage to go. I intend to look evil in the face. I need to see and touch Auschwitz—to make it a reality at a time when it's no longer an emergency. I want my memories to resurface and to make new memories." Although I did my best to defend my decision, Irén simply couldn't fathom why it was so important for me to visit a place of such horror.

Ray and I began our journey by taking an overnight train from Budapest to Poland. We remained awake during much of the night, silently staring out at the darkness surrounding us. The rhythmic chanting of train wheels had almost coaxed me into a state of relaxation when the train came to a stop. Suddenly, heavily armed soldiers abruptly opened our compartment, looked at us scornfully as they checked our papers, and then slammed the door as they left. The harsh sound, reminiscent of the closing of doors on the cattle car, left me chilled to the bone.

As dawn broke, we began to glimpse fields of corn ready for harvest. I told Ray, "We are really going to Auschwitz. It's hard to believe that it's actually happening. It seems fitting that we traveled to Poland in the night, with little sleep, surrounded by darkness. That's how we arrived in the cattle cars. I have such mixed feelings about returning. I'm riding toward the reality of a terrible time in my life. People don't usually return to places where they have suffered." Taking a deep breath, I continued, "But this time I'm going with another person, and I'm free to come and go as I wish, so I shouldn't feel afraid."

After arriving in Kraków and resting for a few hours, we looked for a taxi. Tears stung my eyes as I listened to Ray tell the driver our destination. I began to tremble, wondering what I was doing, dressed up nicely, sitting in a taxi, and listening to Ray ask, "Could you please take us to Auschwitz?" The driver didn't understand English, so I found my voice so I could repeat the request in German. Emotion overwhelmed me, despite my determination to remain composed. It took all my strength to remain calm. I was traveling to the location where the Nazis imprisoned me . . . and where they murdered my mother, grandmother, sister, and baby brother.

Ray later told me that as we began this final leg of our journey, he noticed my white-knuckled grip on the handle of the taxi door and how my gaze seemed fixed on the wedding band I had worn for fifty years. In that moment, I was thinking of my dear husband, the man who stood beside me for decades. I was certain that if Earnest were alive, he would have been holding my hand, encouraging me and telling me he was proud of me for finding the courage to face my fear. I also had no doubt that Earnest's passing was the catalyst for my return. The killing in Auschwitz was the only death I had known intimately until Earnest took his last breath as I held him in my arms; Earnest showed me that death can be peaceful. In a strange way, Earnest's passing helped me realize I needed to return to my family—and that this was the time. The layers of my grief were crossing paths and finally coming together.

The Auschwitz-Birkenau Memorial is a tourist attraction for most of those who visit. However, for me, going there was business. I was suddenly upset that Auschwitz was no more than a way of earning money for the taxi drivers and the so-called tourist buses heading there. More than that, even fifty years after the Holocaust, I was still grappling with the question of why the world stayed silent as Hitler and his followers fanned the flames of bigotry and hate . . . paving the way for the murder of millions. My sudden anger surprised me. I gradually realized that beneath the irritation, I was petrified—all too aware of the painful memories I would soon face. At that moment, it was just too much. I was returning to the place where the Nazis murdered my family, hoping to finally have the freedom to express my grief.

Rain followed us along the route, seemingly aware of the tearful unveiling of my past that awaited me. As we approached our destination, my mood became more serious, almost morose. Looking out the window, I noted the contrast between the rows of modern houses and the ancient church steeples piercing the sky. As the taxi proceeded down a tree-lined road, I noticed a mother pushing her baby in a stroller, and I wondered about the villagers who lived nearby fifty years ago. It felt like a million thoughts were swirling through my mind as I asked Ray, "I wonder if the people who lived around the camp knew what was going on. And if they knew the truth, why did they stay silent while the killing continued?" Although my mind was spinning, I continued, "In the cattle car, we didn't see our surroundings, but now I do. The fields are so fertile here. Is that from the ashes? I wonder how far ashes travel in the wind. And what did the Nazis do with all of the ashes left behind? Look at all of those wildflowers, Ray. Do you think wildflowers are growing inside Auschwitz?"

My thoughts were on my loved ones. It had always been uplifting to remember them, and I wondered if this visit would change my views. Even today, as I think of them, I see them as they were in life. I see their faces, their gestures, their love, and that gives me strength. Sometimes I have a dream where they reach out to me and I run to them, feeling absolute happiness that I am with them once again. I hoped dark memories of their deaths wouldn't surface and replace my peaceful dreams.

I began to think of my sister, Erzsébet, and silently I asked,

Returning

Erzsébet, I wonder what would have happened if I had pulled you into the line with me. Would they have allowed you to stay by my side? Would you have survived? In my mind, I explain to her: *I thought you would be safer in the other line with the mothers and their babies, but you weren't. I'm so sorry you didn't have a chance to enjoy life, because I think you would have enjoyed every minute just like I do.* Aware that Erzsébet would have just turned sixty-four, I turned to Ray and whispered, "Right now Erzsébet would probably be telling me that she would be able to retire in one more year." I continued, "Ray, you're like my little brother, although I can't even imagine what Gábor's face would look like as an adult. My sons were born not long after he was, so you all would be wonderful friends." Family continued to fill my mind as we entered a huge parking lot. The driver turned to us, and with a smile he announced, "We're here."

I asked myself if I was truly ready to go back. I wasn't afraid of Nazis, but I feared the pain of memories. In a way, I had become a prisoner of that fear, and I yearned to be free. The rain suddenly stopped, and the sun emerged from behind the clouds. I had my answer. I was ready.

43

Facing the Fear

Looking around after exiting the taxi, I immediately told Ray, "This isn't the place." We soon discovered we were at the Auschwitz-Birkenau Memorial on the grounds of Auschwitz I, the original Auschwitz camp, not Auschwitz II-Birkenau, the camp where I was imprisoned. The complex, designed to accommodate large groups of tourists by housing a gift store, a cafeteria, a post office, and a booth for purchasing tour tickets, looked far different than it would have during the Nazi era. We walked beyond the commercial complex to some brick prisoner barracks converted into museums honoring Nazi victims and survivors from various countries. We silently read a sign posted for visitors: YOU ARE ENTERING A PLACE OF EXCEPTIONAL HORROR AND TRAGEDY. PLEASE SHOW YOUR RESPECT FOR THOSE WHO SUFFERED AND DIED HERE BY BEHAVING IN A MANNER SUITABLE TO THE DIGNITY OF THEIR MEMORY. I took a deep breath, thinking, *I was a witness to that horror and tragedy. I lived it, and I survived.* I turned to Ray and whispered, "I was there, too. I also deserve respect and dignity. The very fact that I am here is a victory for the human race."

Ray and I eventually found our way to the building that housed the Hungarian museum. We maneuvered down the rickety stairs so we could examine the photographs and historical items housed in the dank basement, a room lit only by a few naked light bulbs and filtered daylight seeping through tiny windows. Several large partitions filled with the names of the approximately 400,000 Hungarians killed by the Nazis stood in the middle of the room. The sheer number was overwhelming. Of the 448,000 Hungarians taken to Auschwitz-Birkenau, only 48,000 of us survived. I reached out to touch the names of my family members, wishing I could bring them back to life. I thought of the millions who perished and how future generations—the unborn children and their children's children— were also lost forever.

Standing beside us was a young woman from Australia. I listened carefully as she told us that her grandparents, natives of Poland, perished in Auschwitz. I wanted to give her a hug, but I resisted, and instead I told her about losing my family, a story I was usually able to share without crying. Yet there in Auschwitz, I was unable to hold back my tears. I felt shaken by my own intense emotions. The young woman kindly reassured me "My goodness, you're a strong woman!" as her tears joined with mine. Before she left, I hugged her, saying, "Thank you for being here and remembering those who died."

I lingered, carefully examining each photograph in hopes of spotting my dear ones. The scenes portrayed in the photos had been my reality. Although I told myself, *Those are only pictures*, and *It happened over fifty years ago*, I was unable to shake the intense despair that engulfed me. I said to Ray, "Look what the Nazis did! That woman sitting on the floor of the cattle car could have been my grandmother, too tired to stand. That woman holding a baby could have been my mother! They were taking pictures as they were ordering us out of the cattle cars and sending people to the gas chambers! Look at those photos of SS women taking prisoners' belongings, with smiles on their faces. What kind of human beings were those people?" I was unprepared for the flood of memories sparked by the photos, including unanticipated relief that the pictures confirmed what I had described to others. The accuracy of my memories was reassuring—an affirmation that the terror buried inside me was real and that I hadn't been somehow misleading myself about the unimaginable horror I had lived through.

Suddenly, a loud, percussive sound startled us, and the lights went out. From the darkness, I heard Ray ask if I was okay. In a calm voice, I answered, "I'm fine, Ray. Now you know what it was like when we were kept in the dark." We peered through the floating specks of dust highlighted by the filtered rays of sun seeping through the narrow windows. Soon the dank cellar seemed to close around us, creating an uncomfortable eeriness. I held tightly to Ray's hand as we cautiously crept toward a dimly lit exit sign and then down a long stairwell, relieved when we finally reached a door. Unfortunately, the massive door wouldn't open even when Ray, who is a big man, pushed against it with all his strength. When the door refused to budge, Ray suggested we retrace our steps and look for another way out.

Unexpected anger engulfed me. I was now a free woman, and I refused to be imprisoned again, even temporarily. I told Ray to move aside, confidently assuring him, "I can open it." I shook the door, attempting to unfasten the large metal latch. Despite my efforts, the door still wouldn't budge. I turned to Ray, declaring, "I'm not a prisoner anymore, and no one can lock me in." Determined not to remain inside a minute longer, I leaned back and gave the door a hefty kick. The door flew open, and daylight engulfed us. Once we walked outside, I triumphantly announced, "We're free!" I felt strong and powerful as we walked into the fresh air and bright sunlight. Wanting to capture the moment, Ray asked me to pose for a picture showing what a free woman looks like. That was easy. I made a "V" for victory sign with both hands and smiled at the camera.

Ray and I spent the next day at the camp that was all too familiar to me—Auschwitz II-Birkenau—entering through the infamous *gate of death*, the fateful endpoint of the train tracks built to accommodate large transports of prisoners destined to die. It was where my family and I arrived in the cattle car, and even on a bright, sunny summer day, it was dark and haunting. I showed Ray where we exited the stifling cattle car after days of imprisonment. I demonstrated the direction we faced while waiting for our turn to stand before Mengele, completely unsuspecting of the horrors to come. I stood there, transfixed by my memories. Reluctantly, I stepped away, reliving those dark moments when the SS forced me to walk away from my dear ones.

Standing before a map of the Birkenau complex, I pointed to my barrack—a single barrack housing 600 people among rows and rows of barracks holding thousands of others. The map left no doubt about the immensity of the Nazi prison. A sign directed us to the path leading to the gas chambers where the Nazis murdered Hungarians throughout the summer of 1944. I peered at the long road traveled by my family before they perished. The road was as empty as could be—a desolate, lifeless path leading to tragedy. I quickly told Ray, "We don't need to walk down that road. It's agonizing enough to see its length and to know the evil awaiting those who walked there. It's a place of pure suffering."

Within minutes, however, I decided I wanted to follow every single step taken by my dear ones, from the train landing all the way to the gas chamber. Stepping away from the spot where I last saw my beloved family, I slowly followed the path they must have traveled. As Ray and I moved forward, I was silent, simply too overwhelmed with emotion to utter a word. In my mind and in my heart, I continued to see my dear ones in those moments when we were last together. I tried not to envision what occurred after we parted. The road was longer than I had imagined, and I wondered how my frail grandmother or my mother recovering from thrombosis could possibly have walked so far. Perhaps the SS transported them in a cart, or perhaps they didn't make it all the way. If so, did the SS force my twelve-year-old sister, Erzsébet, to walk alone? As much as I hope they stayed together, I will never know for sure.

We reached the crematoria at the end of the road. I stopped near the foundation of a destroyed building—Crematorium V—the place where my family and the other Hungarians who arrived on July 1, 1944, were murdered. The building that had housed the gas chamber and crematorium was in ruins, dynamited by the Nazis during the final days of the war in their desperation to destroy evidence of their crimes. As Ray and I stood beside the wreckage, my heart was pounding; tears trickled down my face. I was in the exact location where my dear ones had perished. It took my breath away standing so close to the tragedy that forever changed my life. Although I may have appeared calm on the outside, my insides seemed to be shaking uncontrollably. I tried to push away images of my mother watching her own mother, daughter, and infant son suffocate, while she herself was struggling to breathe. I tried not to wonder if they were screaming or if they were crying. I will never know. However, I hope and pray they didn't suffer long and that the end came quickly.

Looking into the ruins of the crematorium from the outside, I felt paralyzed, unable to move a step closer. Then, suddenly, I lurched forward as if an invisible force reached out and pushed me. Despite feeling dazed by the surreal circumstances, I stepped into the remains of the building, experiencing a desperate need to explore, wanting to find my dear ones somewhere among the rubble. More than that, I wanted to hold them in my arms and comfort them. I staggered through the ruins touching the bricks and cables, trying to become one with the place where they had perished. Engulfed in their pain, I wished I could somehow spirit my dear ones away from that terrible place. I fought an urge to lie down right there in the middle of the decimated crematorium. Sadness coursed through my body and settled in my heart as I recognized the futility of searching for loved ones who no longer existed. In that moment, I fully acknowledged what occurred there fifty years prior. I hoped my dear ones knew I never forgot them and that I had returned to shower them with love.

I was unable to hold back tears and was trembling with the most devastating grief I had ever known. Ray put his arm around me, and we began reciting the ancient Jewish prayer that honors the dead, the Mourner's Kaddish. Although it is a prayer we both know by heart, neither of us had the strength to utter more than a few words.

When we finally walked away, I noticed a black commemorative stone placed beside a nearby pond: TO THE MEMORY OF THE MEN, WOMEN AND CHILDREN WHO FELL VICTIM TO THE NAZI GENOCIDE. HERE LIE THEIR ASHES. MAY THEIR SOULS REST IN PEACE. That was my hope—that the souls of my dear ones were resting in peace, knowing how deeply they were loved.

I had no idea Birkenau was so enormous; as prisoners, other than occasional walks to the disinfection station and our single trip to the site where the Birkenau Orchestra performed, we were restricted to the space surrounding our barrack. Looking around, Ray and I saw the area where row upon row of wooden barracks once stood. Ray and I quietly regarded a plaque at the International Monument to the Victims of Fascism: FOREVER LET THIS PLACE BE A CRY OF DESPAIR AND A WARNING TO HUMANITY, WHERE THE NAZIS MURDERED ABOUT ONE AND ONE HALF MILLION MEN, WOMEN, AND CHILDREN, MAINLY JEWS, FROM VARIOUS COUNTRIES IN EUROPE. I wondered, *Who would have been the Nazi's next victims after all the Jews, Gypsies, homosexuals, and political prisoners were gone?*

As Ray and I walked the entire perimeter of Birkenau, I shook my head in disgust. "Look around you, Ray. Everything you see here focuses on one thing and one thing only. Killing. We are standing in a place of death." We walked for hours . . . thirsty, tired, bitten by bugs. I had forgotten the never-ending swarm of insects. There was no place to sit and no water to drink. We were uncomfortable, but not nearly as uncomfortable as I had been as a prisoner smelling open latrines and choking on the smoke and ash. I remembered so many details. Those memories were burned into my body, my mind, and my soul. How could I possibly forget?

As we walked toward the end of the railroad tracks, I was suddenly overcome with exhaustion and asked Ray if we could rest before continuing. Silence surrounded us as we found our way to the memorial at the end of the far track. While resting, I watched a young tourist carrying a sleeping infant in a backpack. Smiling, I turned to Ray and asked, "Do you see that? Isn't it wonderful that life continues?" Nevertheless, I couldn't help thinking of my baby brother and feeling relief that no one would kill that man's innocent child.

Sitting on the edge of the monument, I thought about my time as a captive, the crimes of the Nazis, and the fate of my dear ones. I felt that by returning to Auschwitz, I was simultaneously liberating my memories as a prisoner and sparking new ideas. This opportunity to look at events from another angle—from the perspective of someone who survived and was now free—unleashed even more poignant recollections yet simultaneously lifted a weight from my shoulders. Although emotionally shaken by the memories flooding my mind and my heart, I celebrated the fact that love of my family had provided me the opportunity to re-experience the details of those heartbreaking days. By having the courage to return to a place of such despair, I was allowing my memories to fully emerge and soar free. I began considering what I wanted to tell people when I got back home. I already had so much to share.

Ray decided he wanted to pick out two small stones from the track where we had stopped to rest, hoping to give one to each of his sons as a remembrance. I was not yet ready to stand, so I asked Ray to also pick up a keepsake for me, pointing to a stone I had spotted and wanted to take home. I was too exhausted to move, so Ray patiently picked up stone after stone until I finally announced, "That's the one!" Ray handed me a smooth, ash-colored talisman shaped like a perfect heart—a representation of eternal love that seemed meant for me. I held the stone tightly in my hand, grasping it as if I were holding on to my loved ones. It was the perfect remembrance of such an emotional day, a memento encapsulating my unwavering love for my dear ones and a symbol that love lives on. After carefully wrapping the stone and placing it in my purse, I was finally ready to resume walking back toward the gate of death.

As we once again stood in the place where I last saw my dear ones, Ray patiently waited for me to decide when it was time to leave. I could imagine myself staying there forever, but I finally admitted, "I'm tired. It's time to go." I looked around me and thought, *Now it's all in my heart.* I promised myself that once I walked away—from the place where my loved ones died and their ashes rested—I wouldn't look back. I feared that if I glanced back even once, I would be unable to leave. I couldn't take that chance . . . so I willed myself to move forward, pretending someone was pushing me in the back. I reminded myself, *You need to go. You have a life waiting for you, and if you leave today, perhaps you can return.* Forcing myself toward the exit, I silently spoke to my loved ones, saying, *I'm so sorry to leave you, but I belong with the living. I must go.*

As we once again walked through the gate of death, I asked Ray to take a picture of me leaving Birkenau. I wanted a memento to remind me of how it felt to be a free woman, leaving that place of horror behind. I was departing with the feeling that I had freed my dear ones, allowing their memories to join me as I returned home.

After my visit to Europe, I was a bundle of emotion. My journey to Auschwitz-Birkenau kept playing in my head, punctuated by a sense that my dear ones were rejoicing because I had finally visited the place where they rested. The details of what happened to my family gave me a lot to consider, moving me well beyond my own misery as a prisoner. My memories, combined with my newfound knowledge, seemed to take on a life of their own—coming forward to surround me, remind me, and tug at my heart. I felt unsettled—as if a UFO had picked me up and transported me to a different planet. Although I love to read, I couldn't find a single book to interest me. I needed quiet—and time to rest and reflect. More than that, I needed a healthy cry. Rather than being connected to my own suffering, my tears stemmed from profound sorrow over the tragic deaths of my dear ones and the other innocents killed by the Nazis. As a prisoner, I had no opportunity to mourn—so it's not surprising that my return to Auschwitz gave rise to an abundance of deeply buried emotions. It was also an opportunity to acknowledge my memories and accept my grief with the overriding recognition that I was a free woman. I also realized I was not only mourning the family I lost in Birkenau, but also my beloved husband. I was missing Earnest, my soul mate, who, before he became ill, was always open to listening to whatever was on my mind. I would have loved to discuss every detail of my return trip to Birkenau.

I wanted to tell Earnest how much my view of the Holocaust had changed since my visit to Poland. It felt like I had spent years attempting to arrange pieces of a mosaic and was finally able to locate the missing parts, put them in place, and consider the whole picture. When I first left Birkenau in 1944, I was still a terrified prisoner, able to view the world only from that lens. As a captive, the SS forced me to look straight ahead, with no more than brief glimpses of what was happening around me. Therefore, when I returned, it was with a prisoner's memory. After learning so much about the enormous camp and the Nazis' activities, I could finally see the whole. And I was no longer afraid. Although my return had been full of heartache—reliving my final moments with my loved ones, following in their footsteps during their last hours on this earth, and visualizing what occurred in the gas chamber—learning the truth of what happened somehow set my soul free. Most importantly, I discovered that I could move in and out of the camp on my own, and kick doors open when I needed to get out. That was a feeling of true freedom. I began to see my survival as a strength—recognizing that after enduring the cruelty of Birkenau, I could survive any challenge.

Spending time on the Birkenau grounds as a free woman allowed me to understand more about the circumstances surrounding my life as a prisoner. Although I will never be able to forget that I was a captive, I began to look at my experiences in a more mature and profound way. Able to see more clearly, my thoughts and emotions became richer and more meaningful. I had been considering my story from the perspective of a prisoner, with a prisoner's memories, but I could now add the perspective of a free woman—not diminishing my recollections of captivity, but instead enhancing them. My return journey to Birkenau allowed my heart to open even wider, moving beyond my own sorrow and understanding more about the many ways people hurt.

44

Again and Again

My visit to Auschwitz-Birkenau made it clear that my dear ones were far, far away—a distance spanning more than fifty years and thousands of miles. Although I no longer felt a need to search for the exact location where they perished, I began considering another trip to Poland, thinking how nice it would be to be close to them once again, if only for a few days. The pull was so strong that I went back seven more times over the next eighteen years, failing to return only when it became too difficult for me to travel such a long distance. I'm not sure how I found the strength to return again and again, but I'm convinced that my visits played an important role in my healing.

Paying tribute to my dear ones at the site where they perished somehow helped to ease my grief. As heartbreaking as it was to see that terrible place, nothing can come close to the moment I learned their fate. And having the opportunity to stand beside the gas chamber and shower them with love seemed to diminish the pain I felt whenever I imagined what they had endured. I never abandoned my most difficult memories, but I was able to enrich them with each visit. Although the Nazis stole my beloved family, the fact that I had the resilience to continue visiting their final resting place shows that life goes on.

Two years after my first visit, shortly before my seventy-fifth birthday, I returned to Auschwitz-Birkenau with my son Steve and his oldest daughter, Rachel, who was then twenty years old, close to my age when I arrived as a prisoner. We first traveled to visit family in Hungary, where Steve and I celebrated the fact that we were together in our homeland for the first time since our escape in 1956. I knew it would be painful to return to Auschwitz again, but I thought I was prepared. Nevertheless, as our taxi passed quaint Polish villages, I once again sat silently, my heart pounding, engulfed in sadness.

As we entered Auschwitz and saw the infamous words ARBEIT MACHT FREI built into the wrought-iron entrance gate, I adamantly disagreed, "Work will make you free? That was a lie! Nobody got free in Auschwitz!" Once again, it was heartbreaking to explore Birkenau, standing where the cattle car stopped and where Mengele separated me from my loved ones. We walked the long distance to the remains of the barrack where I had been a prisoner, where nothing more than the foundation of the building remained. Our final stop was at Crematorium V, where my dear ones perished. Standing side by side, blanketed in sorrow, Steve, Rachel, and I recited the Mourner's Kaddish—praying for the family we lost and for each of the innocent souls who died under such terrible circumstances. This time, surrounded by family, I was able to say the words of the sacred prayer.

Rachel wandered into a nearby field, picking a small bouquet of delicate, white wildflowers; her eyes brimming with tears, she bowed her head as she gently placed the flowers on the black commemorative marker. Steve, Rachel, and I held on to each other, three generations of tears moistening the sacred soil. I spoke up, mentioning that Earnest and I had not only survived, but we also created a wonderful family—a loving family—that was something far different from what Hitler had intended. I knew Earnest would be proud that I was standing there paying tribute to my dear ones with our son and granddaughter standing beside me—a continuation of love and life that represented a triumph over the Nazi hatred.

Seven years later, Steve and I again returned to Europe, this time with Steve's youngest daughter, Miriam. We first visited Budapest, savoring the brisk fall air and the trees adorned with colorful leaves. We eagerly explored the city, riding the old-fashioned streetcars I remember from my youth. I showed Miriam the store where Steve asked if Stalin was a criminal, and I climbed the familiar four flights of stairs so she could see the apartment where we lived before our escape. Perhaps because I was eighty-two, Miriam remarked on my endurance as we walked for miles exploring familiar places. I imagine my pride in the beauty of the city spurred me on.

Miriam enjoyed visiting Earnest's brother, Sándor, and his wife and seeing how Hungarians live. In this case, she saw her relatives (an economist with a Ph.D. married to a medical doctor specializing in pulmonology) living on a limited income in a very modest apartment, beautified with woodwork constructed by Sándor himself. We also met with Sándor's son Miklos, someone who had enjoyed an elevated position in the Communist government before it collapsed in 1989. I have to say Miklos didn't seem pleased with our visit. When I asked him about changes in Hungary since the end of communism fifteen years earlier, he was pessimistic about the future of the country, complaining that there were beggars on the streets and worries about losing employment, even for those who performed well. I guess his attitude made sense since he had enjoyed many privileges under the Communist regime.

Miriam was delighted to meet my stepmother Irén, whom she described as sweet and adorable. Although they couldn't easily communicate, Miriam and Irén reveled in each other's company, with Irén frequently laughing as Miriam sat beside her holding her hand and listening intently to stories about Steve when he was a child. Irén kept mentioning how much she liked Miriam, and attempted to talk her into remaining in Hungary, suggesting that she could introduce Miriam to a nice Jewish boy. She then sweetened her offer with promises of delicious Hungarian desserts. Irén mentioned how much Miriam reminded her of me when I was Miriam's age. I wasn't surprised because I see those similarities myself. In fact, Miriam followed in my footsteps and became an elementary school teacher.

Irén, determinedly navigating the uneven cemetery ground using her cane for support, led us to my father's grave—a solemn moment for Miriam who never had a chance to meet her great-grandfather. When Irén purchased my father's headstone, she decided to also have the names of my mother, brother, and sister carved into the granite. Miriam placed a small stone on the grave—a symbol that she had come to honor my father and the others—and then solemnly kissed the ground where her great-grandfather was buried. Miriam has a close relationship with Steve, just as I was close to my dear father, so she understood the depth of my grief as we stood beside the place of my father's burial.

This time we rented a car to make the journey to Auschwitz-Birkenau, enjoying the beautiful drive through the hills of Slovakia and admiring the breathtaking fall colors and the tiny houses with smoke gently billowing from the chimneys. Miriam loves to sing, so she led us in song as we drove the route to Poland. When we visited the Hungarian museum in Auschwitz, I was pleased to see a group of Hungarian high school students learning about the Holocaust. I told them I was a survivor, shared a bit of my story, and thanked them for taking the time to learn what occurred during the Nazi reign. It warmed my heart to meet students who were so kind, caring, and interested in learning about that dark period of Hungarian history.

In the summer of 2006, sixty-two years after I arrived in the cattle car, I had the wonderful experience of traveling to Hungary and Poland with my son Steve and his middle daughter, Julia, together with Professor Jim Lortz from Western Washington University. Jim had decided to make a documentary of my life, focusing on my early years in addition to my time in the Auschwitz II-Birkenau and Münchmühle camps. Jim and I first met when he was directing a student production of *The Diary of Anne Frank*, and he invited me to speak to the cast. Jim told me his students poured their hearts into the production after hearing my story. Jim and I had an instant connection, and he sometimes told people, "If Noémi likes you, it's like you have a shoe in the door." I guess he had a shoe in my door, because I liked Jim a lot and was grateful for his interest in my story.

While we were in Hungary, we explored Szeged, the beautiful city where Steve and I were born and where Earnest and I were married. We then traveled to Debrecen to see the house where my family lived before the Nazis took us away, now no more than a pile of rubble overgrown with vegetation. I was able to locate a house with similar features, including large windows, a heavy wooden door, and an attic with small openings similar to those that Erzsébet and I peered through during our final days in the ghetto. Jim, who was following me everywhere as he filmed the documentary, teased me about how the Hungarian in me came alive as I absorbed the energy of the country. He joked that wherever we went, I was always teaching—giving one history lesson after the other.

While visiting the Budapest Holocaust Memorial Center, we stood in silence before a metal sculpture of a weeping willow tree filled with leaves, each engraved with the name of a Hungarian Holocaust victim—so many leaves, each symbolizing a life lost. I listened as a teacher chaperoning a group of Israeli youth told her students, "That was a long time ago. Israel is the future." Hearing her dismissive tone, I felt a need to speak up. I faced the students and told them I was a survivor, explaining, "It's important to honor the Jews who suffered during the Holocaust. We can't forget them." Although the chaperone gave me a look making it clear she wasn't pleased with my commentary, I continued, "We need to respect those who died and suffered. Understanding what happened during the Holocaust doesn't take away from the future of Israel. Instead, understanding history will give strength to future generations."

I was pleased to have an opportunity to tell my story in Hungarian during a visit to a local university. I have to admit, I was nervous speaking to a Hungarian audience about historical realities such as the cruelty of the Hungarian Arrow Cross. Nevertheless, it was worth the anxiety, and I was proud of myself for taking on the challenge. It was important for those students to hear the story, and I appreciated their thoughtful questions. It was not an easy conversation, at least not for me, as I struggled to hide my disappointment that the Hungarian people didn't intervene when the Arrow Cross came for us. Of course, I did my best to make sure the students didn't feel guilty, pointing out that the Holocaust happened long before they were born.

Our next stop was the Auschwitz II-Birkenau Memorial in Poland, where we were joined by a group of Washington State teachers who had come to hear my story of the Holocaust in the place where it occurred. Traveling to Auschwitz as a free woman and as an educator, I felt six feet tall. It was a privilege for me—and another step in my healing—to be able to discuss Auschwitz with the teachers, answering their questions and sharing my experiences and what I had learned. I appreciated every moment I spent with those dedicated educators who took time out of their summer to witness Auschwitz. It was also special to have my dear granddaughter Julia on our journey. I could see in everyone's eyes a true understanding of the depth of the tragedy as we explored the museums and viewed remnants of the Nazi cruelty—museum cases filled with shoes, glasses, prayers shawls, empty cans of the Zyklon B used in the gas chambers, and piles of human hair. As we stood before the evidence of Nazi atrocities, I implored those dear teachers to always remember what happens when hatred, prejudice, and bigotry flourish and no one speaks up.

It was frustrating to listen to our tour guides dispassionately recite statistics about the number of people murdered and other details of the Nazi cruelty, almost forgetting that each victim was a living human being. I wondered, *Do they truly understand the horror that happened here?* I know the guides were only doing their job, but I just couldn't understand how it was possible to conduct a tour involving such intense sadness and loss with so little emotion. When the tour guides told us that the people who lived nearby were unaware of what was happening, it took all of my strength not to challenge them by asking, "Didn't they smell the stench of death and see the fire and the falling ash?" I again stayed silent rather than argue when I asked a tour leader if the Allies could have saved lives by bombing the railway lines leading to Auschwitz, and he only reluctantly acknowledged that perhaps it was a mistake not to intervene.

The teachers decided to explore an exhibit that included a reconstruction of the original Auschwitz gas chamber. At first, I told the group that I preferred to wait in the fresh air, but later decided that perhaps I should venture inside, just for a minute. I took the hand of Liz, one of the teachers, and held on to her as we slowly stepped inside. We stood together in silence for a few seconds, but almost immediately, I felt an urgent need to leave. It felt like my heart would explode with grief as my mind filled with thoughts of my loved ones' last minutes on this earth. Once outside, I turned to Liz, who had kindly stayed beside me, and quietly assured her, "I'm glad I went in." I needed to know.

My granddaughter Julia remained by my side as we walked to the ruins of Crematorium V in Birkenau. Steve and I once more said Kaddish, with Julia and other Jewish members of our group solemnly joining in our prayer. As I have done each visit, I hugged the cold commemorative stone, the closest I can come to giving my dear ones a final embrace. As he filmed, Jim quietly commented that

Again and Again

Auschwitz-Birkenau felt like holy ground inhabited by the souls of all who had perished there, each of them saying loudly and clearly, "Don't forget us."

The following spring, I finally had the opportunity to share my experience with my younger son, George, when he made his first visit to Auschwitz. Jim and Ray once again joined me. George was touched by all he saw and expressed how much the visit deepened his understanding of the meaning of suffering, hate, and prejudice. He smiled when, on May 22, 2007, I wrote in the Auschwitz visitor book, "I am here again as a free woman!" We also visited the German Holocaust Archive in the tranquil town of Bad Arolsen, where I was shocked to hold the faded piece of paper that I had signed the day I arrived at Birkenau. It took my breath away to see my signature—the handwriting of an innocent young woman just beginning to recognize the absolute cruelty of the Nazi regime. Feeling as if it was scorching my hand, I held the card only briefly before abruptly pushing it away toward the German women assisting us, whose tears showed they understood the depth of my emotion. It eased my distress to see they cared.

During each of the eight visits I made to Auschwitz as a free woman, I had the company of family and dear friends. I will never forget how each person stood beside me—supporting and holding me up during those emotional visits to a tragic time in my past. Having my sons and three of my grandchildren accompany me to Auschwitz-

223

Birkenau provided me with a sense of continuity and an assurance that our family history and the lessons of the Holocaust will remain alive. It meant so much to have them join me, lovingly paying their respects to the family they never met and honoring the millions of other innocents who perished alongside them. I hope the story of these visits will pass from generation to generation.

45

Sharing and Healing

Although I sometimes told my sixth-grade students about escaping communism, I never spoke about the Holocaust publicly until after I retired. For years, I reacted with fear if someone asked about my religion. I never denied being Jewish, but I would answer as quietly as possible, looking around to see if anyone was listening. I couldn't forget the consequences of being Jewish in Europe nor shake the feeling that something terrible would happen if people learned my religion. I would sometimes ask myself, *What are you afraid of?* Whether it was a real fear or an imagined fear, it doesn't matter. Fear is fear.

My public discussions began when I shared my story with a small group at our synagogue in Bellingham. Soon afterward, a friend of our rabbi, the pastor of a local Methodist Church, asked me to speak to his congregation. Although I accepted the invitation, to say I was terrified doesn't begin to describe my trepidation. I had to pull together every ounce of courage to stand in front of a group of strangers and describe the heartbreaking events that forever changed my life. Once I began to speak, however, I could feel the compassion from everyone listening. Moreover, once I started telling my story, I couldn't stop talking. I had so much to say.

Earnest is the one who had encouraged me to accept that first speaking invitation, confident that I could use my teaching skills to help people learn about history. When I was hesitant, Earnest asked, "Why not give it a try and see how it goes? I'll be with you every step of the way." That convinced me. After my talk, when I agreed to an interview with a local newspaper reporter, I suddenly panicked, thinking, *Oh boy! What will happen once people know I'm Jewish?* Although I was anxious about the interview, with Earnest's support, I faced my fear.

Once the article appeared in the newspaper, nothing terrible happened. Instead, I began receiving invitations to speak at schools, churches, and community groups. I was once again nervous, wondering if it was safe to continue telling my story. The memories of living under the Nazis and Soviets, buried deep inside me, were seeping into the present. Yet I realized the importance of people hearing directly from a Holocaust survivor. And that was the beginning. Although it took me forty years to feel comfortable sharing my story, I now realize that being a survivor brings responsibilities—a duty to give testimony about what I witnessed. I want people to understand the circumstances that led to the Holocaust. I want to help ensure that civilized people never again succumb to hate.

Sharing and Healing

When I returned from my first visit to Auschwitz-Birkenau, I was more determined than ever to teach the lessons of the Holocaust to young and old. I accepted every invitation that came my way—from civic and church groups to elementary schools, secondary schools, and universities—hoping to share my experiences with as many people as possible. I was clear about my purpose: to educate people to the dangers of prejudice, discrimination, and hate by sharing my personal example of what occurred in Europe. I was determined to do whatever I could to erase ignorance, apathy, and denial. I also wanted people, especially those who have experienced trauma, to know that it is possible to heal the pain.

I found myself changing and growing as I shared my story. I began to feel more urgency to speak about societal concerns and about problems that those in the audience might be experiencing in their daily lives. If we have truly learned the lessons of the Holocaust, we cannot ignore the hurts and injustices that surround us, nor forget the lessons of past injustices such as slavery, the killing and forced relocation of Indigenous people, or the treatment of Japanese Americans during World War II. We need to remember the lessons of history as we consider the political context of current events throughout the world.

As I moved forward with my own healing, I realized I had an opportunity to help other survivors of trauma. I often listened to quietly shared confidences and responded to letters sent to me. All of this opened my eyes and my heart to the fact that, although the Holocaust is unique in its horror, many people have experienced trauma and loss in their own lives. There are many who hurt—so I began to focus on encouraging those listening to my testimony to open their hearts to all who suffer and who have a need to feel heard.

I believe that those of us who have lived through challenging experiences can benefit from sharing our stories, at least with friends, family, or trusted professionals. I have no doubt that the thousands of people who have honored me by listening to me speak have helped me heal. Every single time I talk about my experiences, it never fails that I go back in time and practically relive each of the difficult moments. It is a trauma, a tragedy, full of fear and pain. My emotions are fresh, and listeners are able to see through my eyes. Even children who have difficulty paying attention listen carefully and relate to what I am saying, sometimes telling me, "I was there with you. I could see it in my mind." Sharing my story has given me strength, and that has allowed my fear and despair to transform to courage. When I look into the eyes of people in the audience, I see their compassion and sympathy, and I feel their love.

When I share my story, I stress that we should take care not to generalize—not all Germans were Nazis, nor did all Germans take part in what happened during Hitler's reign. If we generalize and look at certain people negatively without knowing them, we're doing the same as the Nazis. I make sure people understand that most Germans were not killers. In fact, many Germans disagreed with Hitler's actions and risked their lives by taking a stand against his racist beliefs. I also understand that many Germans are still carrying the pain of their country's connection to a leader who managed to lead so many people astray during that terrible time.

In high schools, there are sometimes exchange students from

Sharing and Healing

Germany in the audience. I ask to talk to them before my speech, explaining that I have a story that might be difficult to hear and assuring them they shouldn't feel guilty: "Your parents weren't alive when this happened. I want you to listen so you can learn about the Nazis, and then I hope you will tell your parents and your grandparents that you met a Holocaust survivor who does not hate. You can help them understand the lessons of the Holocaust. And if you encounter racism or hate anywhere in the world, I hope you will find the courage to speak up rather than ignore what you have witnessed." I watch those students in the audience and see their tears, and I hold out my arms when they come for a hug.

I have had the honor of speaking to many wonderful audiences, and the listeners are always respectful, attentive, and eager to learn. I have traveled to speak in a number of states and as far away as Taiwan, where I spent several days with students and community members when I was eighty-seven years old. Soon after my Taiwan adventure, I spoke at a Daughters of the American Revolution (DAR) conference where they honored me with the DAR Americanism Medal. I was quite nervous, but the huge audience gave me a standing ovation, so I must have done okay despite my nerves. I also traveled to Montana to speak in a community concerned about local neo-Nazi activity and have also had the privilege of speaking at university graduations. And I will never forget the time I spoke at the Whidbey Island Naval Air Station; I was so excited to be in front of American military members that I concluded by telling the group that I wished

I could embrace each of them to thank them for their service. To my surprise, most of the audience lined up for a hug.

I have spoken at the federal prison in Monroe, Washington, and at our local jail. When I speak to people who are incarcerated, I can see they understand what it means to be a prisoner. The message I always want them to hear is that they still have a chance to make changes in their lives. Some women cry as they hear my story, and I can tell they truly understand my message that there is hope even after something terrible happens. The men shed no tears, but I can see they are with me, looking at me intently and sometimes nodding. Afterward, seeing my gray hair and the face of a grandmother, all of the women and some of the men get in line for a hug. And I'm happy to take the time to give each one a big embrace.

My long life has been a gift and has allowed me to continue sharing my story. Just before my ninety-sixth birthday, I looked at the notebook where I have kept a list of each speaking engagement—sometimes a classroom of thirty children and sometimes an auditorium filled with hundreds. To my astonishment, I had already shared my story 1,222 times. When people call me now, they sound more hesitant when they ask if I am still speaking to groups. However, I always answer, "Of course I am, but you'll need to pick me up and take me home." I also let them know that I will be taking my Cadillac with me—that's what I call the bright red walker that I use to keep me steady when I move from place to place.

World War II is history, and important lessons come from history. As long as I'm alive, I plan to continue sharing what I witnessed—the stories of my loved ones and so many others. Everything that happened during the Holocaust is a heavy load to carry, but I am determined not to allow that weight to stop me or slow me down. The memories that I hold on to, the ones closest to my heart, are the memories that give me the strength to do all I can to make sure it never happens again. That is the story I want to share. The people lost in the Holocaust can remain in the hearts of this and future generations if we take the time to hear the sad truth. Just as I'm honoring my loved ones by speaking publicly, everyone who hears my story is also honoring them, allowing those who were with us yesterday to remain with us today.

46

Messages of Love, Hope, and Healing

I f there is any positive aspect to significant life challenges, it is the lessons we learn. I saw what hate, bitterness, and anger look like and the damage they can do. It is the wisdom I have gathered from these experiences that I want to share in this final chapter of my story.

Embracing Hope and Moving Forward

I feel fortunate that I was not only able to survive the Holocaust, but that I also have been able to heal and lead a purpose-filled life, perhaps made more meaningful by the unexpected tragedies I faced. I have no doubt that my experiences made me a stronger person. In my situation, you might imagine I would prefer to forget what I went through. Yet to forget would mean throwing out part of my life, including valuable lessons and treasured memories of my dear ones. Instead, to remain whole, it has been crucial for me to accept the reality of the tragedy and the emotions of those difficult times. I needed to recognize that my traumatic memories are part of who I am. I wish the Holocaust never happened, but life is the whole package, and I have no choice but to live with the hand I was dealt.

I must admit that I'm not always happy and smiling, especially if there is a big bump in the road. After encountering a difficult situation, it helps me to talk about what happened, recognize my feelings, discover the lessons, and then decide how I can most effectively use what I learned to better my life or the lives of others. When I feel upset, I hold on to hope by remembering that tomorrow is a new day. Hope is a door you can walk through. You don't know what's on the other side, but it's important to keep the door open. If you close it, you'll never know what you might have found.

It took me a while to realize how deeply people connect with my story; perhaps that connection occurs because so many of us have encountered significant challenges. Someone else's suffering might be different from mine as a Holocaust survivor, but I recognize that many people carry burdens. I would never say—nor do I believe— that my experiences were more damaging or difficult than events faced by someone else. Trauma is trauma. We should take every person's trauma seriously and deal with it compassionately. I am hopeful that my story will help other survivors of tragedy realize that even when it takes a while to get over the immediate effects of trauma, there is life and there is hope—especially when you find the courage to allow your feelings to come to the surface.

We all face challenges, and we each need to decide how to respond to events in our lives, especially when what has occurred is horrific. We must consider whether we want to spend our energy looking back on the past with despair or looking ahead with optimism. If you are suffering due to past or present events in your life, please remember there is a way forward—as long as you hold on to the possibility of a brighter future. If possible, find someone you trust so you can share your pain. No matter how horrific your memories or how isolated you may feel, please know there are people who care.

No matter how much distress or trouble you are experiencing, it's not too late to rediscover your power and recapture hope. Even on those days where you feel overwhelmed, I hope you will realize you are stronger than you think. If you dive deep enough to find the resilience within you, it will allow you not only to heal, but also to blossom and to grow. You can do it! In fact, you may come out stronger than ever. I'm proof of that.

If you have become buried in hurt, it's not too late to dig your way out. You'll see that it's quite possible to carry happiness alongside recollections of suffering. It's also possible to use your experience for good—educating or encouraging others by sharing your story. You can use what you have learned about survival to reach out to other people going through a hard time and then celebrate each opportunity you have to help someone heal.

I firmly believe that strength and joy can arise from pain and distress. Although it's not possible to undo the past, those of us who have survived trauma can refuse to allow tragic events to hold us back and further compound our pain. And if we don't permit past misery to define us, we can heal by reimagining our future, recapturing joy, and celebrating life.

Focusing on Love Rather than Hate

I imagine that my story has opened your eyes to the ease with which hatred can grow and destroy. Hate can be perilously insidious, beginning as a seedling that grows into a powerful tree, and before we know it, we are surrounded by a dark and dangerous forest. Hate can destroy a person, or can destroy a civilization. Why is it so easy for some people to hate their fellow human beings? We asked that question when imprisoned in Auschwitz, trying to understand why the Nazis hated us when they didn't even know us. Similarly, we may ask why some people hold so much animosity toward certain groups even in today's world.

I wish we could remove the word *hate* from our vocabulary, and even avoid using it in daily conversation. When I hear someone use the word in reference to hating something or someone, I always wonder, *Do they really mean what they are saying?* When we use it so casually, it's easy to forget the strength of the word or what happens when we allow hate to flourish.

I realize my reaction to what happened during the Holocaust could easily have been hatred. Many trauma survivors find it difficult to let go of their anger or resentment. I feel fortunate that I not only survived, but that I also avoided becoming bitter. I learned in Auschwitz what hate can do, and I refused to do to myself what the Nazis did to me. If I focused on hating the Nazis, then I would still be their prisoner. I would be unable to create a peaceful life if I lived with hate. Some people wonder if I have forgiven the Nazis. Although I am working on it, I doubt I will ever be able to say that I have completely forgiven them. Nevertheless, when someone asks if I hate the Nazis for what they did to my family, I can honestly say I don't hate anyone. I feel sadness, anger, and hurt, but not hate. There is another way to live life, and that has always been my choice—to live with love.

Despite the fact that I have seen the ugliest side of humanity, I have hope for the future. I believe that we can work together to ensure that we never allow hate to gain a foothold in this beautiful world. I realize that those who spew hate have somehow been taught to hate. I also believe that attitudes can change.

Celebrating Freedom

Speaking as a Holocaust survivor and a woman who lived under two dictatorships, I recognize that freedom is precious—a gift we should cherish. To me, something as simple as sipping water represents freedom. My favorite beverage in the whole world is clean, cool water. Never forgetting living conditions during the Holocaust, I celebrate that I am able to drink water early in the morning, during the day, or in the middle of the night. When speaking publicly about the conditions when I was a prisoner, I often feel parched—so I stop and slowly take a sip of water, realizing how lucky I am to have the freedom to quench my thirst.

Freedom comes with responsibility. It's important to preserve our freedom by taking the time to vote and by recognizing that some politicians attempt to achieve power by undermining democracy. To me, casting a ballot is a privilege because I lived in a country where elections were rigged and our votes were meaningless. I treasure the fact that here in America I am free to express my opinions about the government without fear of punishment. In Hungary, if I had dared to share my thoughts publicly, I would have ended up in jail. After having my life forever changed by the whims of authoritarian leaders, it's difficult for me to watch some of the things happening in the world today. It feels all too familiar. When the Nazi and Communist leaders told lies, many people believed their propaganda. They used lies to dehumanize my family and my Jewish friends. Truth is an essential ingredient in daily life and in a true democracy. At least in this century, we have many ways to check to see if what we hear is true.

Speaking Up and Spreading Kindness

I am hopeful that reading my story will help people understand the dangers of prejudice and discrimination, and the importance of making sure we don't overlook or minimize oppressive behaviors when we see them. We need to listen for dehumanizing words and act to protect those who some may dehumanize—remembering we are all human beings. I recall how deeply it hurt when the Nazis came to Hungary and people began to look at us with contempt and refer to us using racial slurs and unkind words. I know that many people have been hurt in a similar way by prejudice and cruel words. I am hopeful that by acknowledging these realities and focusing on creating a society where everyone is treated with respect, we will begin to heal these deep wounds.

We need to recognize that actions that may seem relatively minor, like name-calling or cruel joking, must be addressed. They are not only hurtful, but they are also dangerous because words can subtly sow the seeds of hatred. If we see injustice and discrimination, we can't afford to say, "Don't worry. It will pass." We can't wait quietly for the situation to improve because things may become worse rather than better. Perhaps the tragedy of the Holocaust could have been prevented if the Germans, the Poles, the Hungarians, and the rest of the world had taken a strong stand against Nazism. I also wish that we, the Jewish people, had stood up to the Nazis before their actions led to such incredible suffering. There was talk about resisting, but compliance was the norm. It felt impossible to do anything other than obey the increasingly authoritarian rules. Now, however, I have no doubt that I would speak out. I understand the consequences of remaining silent.

My experiences taught me that we cannot blindly follow people in power, especially if they say hateful things or try to turn groups against each other. We must do all we can so that ridicule, cruelty, and disrespect never become acceptable or, even worse, become the norm. We may want to deny that prejudice and racist behavior happen in our current world, but they do. Will future generations one day look back at twenty-first-century violence and aggression, wondering why we just stood by? And, sadly, the divide between people appears to be growing. Here in the United States, we have had destruction and killing in sacred places of worship—synagogues, churches, and mosques. Even in my own community, vandals have toppled tombstones in our Jewish cemetery, put up Nazi posters, and destroyed Jewish Studies books in our university library. These are all red flags—events that we cannot ignore.

People often ask me, "So what can I do to make a difference?" Although no one person can change the world, we can each examine our actions, deciding on small steps we individually can take to show people we care. We can do our best to be a good listener whenever we are with someone who needs to talk. We can step forward whenever we have an opportunity to be of service. When a child or adult has a terrible hurt—such as domestic violence, physical or sexual abuse, distressing interactions with people in authority—we can be the one to listen to their story, believe in them, show them love, and give them hope. We can demonstrate respect for everyone we meet, and speak up if we see someone bullying or disrespecting other people. We can teach the children in our lives the importance of empathy and respect. We can be free with smiles toward friends and strangers alike, spreading caring and compassion wherever we go. I have faith in humankind, and it warms my heart when I see people taking actions to ensure that love prevails.

Living with Gratitude

Being alive is a gift—especially for anyone who has lived through danger—so I focus on celebrating life. I recognize how precious each day truly is. I continually attempt to emphasize the positive and treasure each minute I spend with family and friends. I try to live with gratitude for the simple things in life. Perhaps because of the suffering I endured, I don't take anything for granted and do my best not to spend my precious time worrying or complaining.

I have been very blessed. When I was young, I had parents who were devoted to my well-being. Friends and family continue to encircle me with their love. It hasn't always been easy, but I have had a wonderful life. I am grateful for the fulfillment I found as a wife, mother, and teacher. My sons, Steve and George, have grown into exceptional men whom I can always count on. Their amazing wives, Jan and Pat, became the daughters I never had. Jan has lovingly cared for me, always with the compassion of a daughter toward a mother, and when Pat comes to visit, she showers me with love. I have wonderful grandchildren and adorable great-grandchildren.

As a member of the last generation able to speak about the Holocaust from personal experience, I feel grateful to the many people who have listened to my personal testimony, allowing me to honor my family and the millions of innocent people killed by the Nazis. I have tried to build a memorial to my dear ones, using love and kindness as the foundation and empathy, compassion, and wisdom as the building blocks. I sincerely hope the lessons I have shared will live on long after I am gone, perhaps making a positive change in the world. I remain optimistic that those of you who understand my message will step up and do whatever you can to make the world a safer and more compassionate place.

Afterword

My Dear Friend's Legacy of Love

Each of us has a life story to share—an opportunity to bless those who come after us with our love and wisdom. I have no doubt that Noémi's intention in working on this project was not only to bear witness to the Holocaust, but also to impart the lessons she learned from her experiences and to help others navigate their own challenges.

Despite Noémi's dedication to finishing this book, and her delight as she read each page of the manuscript, unexpected obstacles slowed our progress. Each incident provided me with a glimpse into Noémi's strength and unflappable attitude as she used hope and optimism to move forward.

I saw firsthand how Noémi faced tragedy when, on October 27, 2018, the massacre at the Tree of Life Synagogue occurred. Already concerned about recent increases in racially motivated violence and white supremacist sentiment, Noémi's normally cheerful voice was filled with sadness as she discussed the tragedy in Pittsburgh, asking, "Haven't we gone through enough? Do we have to go through this now, here in the United States? One day it's an attack on people praying in a church or a mosque, and now it's the killing of people worshiping in a synagogue. Hate took the lives of those innocent people, and hate took them away from their families. What is going on? Will we ever see an end to hate? We need to do something to make it stop! This lets me know that I need to continue speaking. And I'm glad that you're continuing to write. We are both doing something that can make a difference. We need to do all that we can to make the world a more peaceful place."

Although we had no specific deadline, Noémi and I were both well aware that our time for working on this book together might be limited. About three months after we began, in late December of 2018, I arrived at Noémi's home at my scheduled time and was concerned when Noémi didn't answer the door. I let myself into her house with a key she had given me decades before—a key I had never used but had decided to keep in my car "just in case." Once inside, I discovered Noémi had fainted, hitting her head when she fell. She was taken to the hospital, where the doctors eventually stabilized her heart rhythm with a pacemaker.

When Noémi returned home, her left arm in a sling, she needed round-the-clock assistance. In typical Noémi fashion, she approached the month-long period of recovery with humor and gratitude, telling me, "I don't feel like myself yet, but I'm thankful my heart is still beating. I'm actually lucky I passed out. My heart was in bad shape, but that was the warning that allowed me to get it fixed. I can't do everything I want to do right now, but this isn't a tragedy."

During those weeks, I spent many hours with Noémi. Although frustrated by her physical limitations, Noémi's resilience was apparent as she pushed herself to regain her independence, celebrating each small victory. She cheerfully chatted with me during each visit and was not surprised when I continued to take notes. "Being sick isn't me, but now, all of a sudden, it's become me—whether I like it or not. I need to appreciate what I'm able to do, instead of feeling upset about the things I can't do. People who fall into despair lose their chance to enjoy life. I can't let that happen to me. I never realized my left arm was so important, but from now on, I'll be sure to appreciate it every day! And when this is all over, we'll have a big celebration to honor my arm. Even being able to wash the dishes is part of life and something I'll also celebrate once I'm strong enough to stand at the sink again. This whole situation is absolutely unbelievable; it came on uninvited, but I'm learning to be patient. What else can I do? I'm really hurting right now, but I need to accept that I have pain and then do my best to deal with it. I'm determined to get better because I like to be active, but I realize it's up to me—so I'll do everything possible to become strong again. I'm still alive, and I want to stay that way, so once I'm able to move around, I'll take care not to do anything too risky."

As Noémi recovered, her cardiologist mentioned the possibility of replacing her diseased heart valve, carefully outlining the potential risks for someone ninety-six years of age. Noémi had strong opinions about the possibility of surgery. "To me, being alive is not about continuing to exist but instead about making the most of every day. I look out my window and see the beauty of nature. I enjoy my food, and I enjoy my family and friends. Life has so many good points to it. It's a reality that I could be gone tomorrow. If that's true, I want to spend my time making the most of my life. It makes no sense for me to sit and worry about how much longer I will live. I won't let concern about my future spoil the present. I still have work to do!" Noémi once more poured her heart into working with me on the book and was eventually strong enough to continue her public speaking.

The spring of 2019 continued, and so did our work. One Sunday afternoon in May, Noémi and her son Steve attended a concert highlighting an Israeli pianist who came to perform with our local symphony orchestra. When I stopped by her house the next morning, Noémi was still relishing the experience, telling me, "The music at yesterday's concert was magical. I felt it in my heart. Listening to beautiful music is such a gift!" In typical Noémi fashion, minutes later she was concentrating on telling her story online to a class of middle school students in Denver. That Tuesday, Noémi traveled to speak to another group of middle school students in a neighboring county, and on Thursday, after a ninety-minute drive, she shared her story with approximately 250 eighth graders, taking time afterward to give hugs and to pose for photos.

The next day, after a busy week doing what she loved, Noémi ran into an obstacle that even she was unable to overcome; she entered our local intensive care unit with congestive heart failure. When I saw her in the hospital the next day, Noémi's first words to me were: "We'll have to put this in the book!" Each time I visited the hospital, after directing my attention to the multitude of flowers, cards, and letters that decorated her room, she asked, "Are you still writing?"

On the morning of June 7, Noémi suddenly lost consciousness. Steve, who was working at a clinic on one of the San Juan Islands, flew back to Bellingham, joining his wife, two of their daughters, and their Zimbabwean exchange-student daughter at Noémi's bedside. With no hope of recovery, close friends and the rabbi assembled around Noémi's bedside, surrounding her with love, music, and prayers. George called from Ohio, solemnly telling Noémi that she was a wonderful mother, grandmother, and human being, and that it was okay for her to go. In that moment, Noémi seemed to smile.

At the very same time we were saying our farewells, a group of parents and teachers gathered at our local Catholic school. Unaware of Noémi's impending death, they celebrated Noémi's dedication to Holocaust education at their school, awarding her the school's annual Volunteer of the Year Award. We were all honoring an extraordinary woman who had made a difference in countless lives.

Noémi's funeral illustrated the strength of her love and her spirit.

Hundreds filled the synagogue. Speakers reminisced about Noémi's tremendous influence on their lives—as a teacher, friend, mother, and grandmother. The entire service was an uplifting remembrance of Noémi's messages of love, hope, and perseverance. Hearing heart-felt stories about Noémi was a vivid reminder that it is possible for joy to spring from darkness.

As the first of many speakers, Steve and George spoke poignant-ly and humorously about their mother. George ended his eulogy by singing "Wind Beneath My Wings," the song he had chosen for the mother-son dance at his wedding. His voice broke when he came to the final lyrics.

Noémi's granddaughter Miriam, a teacher and a lover of music like her grandmother, also brought us to tears as she played her gui-tar and sang a song she had written and dedicated to Noémi. The sound of the gentle melody lingered as Miriam sang the final lyrics:

I'll tell you a story, I'll tell you with my heart
I won't leave out the sadness and I'll keep the joyful parts
You'll hold me closely, with a love in your eyes
And I'll be filled up . . . you'll be filled up . . . we'll be filled up.

Noémi's oldest grandchild, Rachel, also captured the essence of Noémi's remarkable life as she read portions of a letter she had writ-ten while Noémi was in the hospital. "Grandma, when I think of you, I don't think of a hospital bed. I think of energy and life. I treasure the wonderful memories of all of the time you spent with me, including our visit to Auschwitz and Budapest, one of the most meaningful experiences ever. Through your appreciation of life, your strength, and your resilience, you have taught me never to take anything for granted. You are and always will be the strongest person I'll ever have the privilege of knowing. I appreciate that you've always made me feel loved and encouraged me by telling me I'm a good mother. It has been such a joy introducing you to my children—your great-grand-children—and watching your face explode with love every time we visit."

Rachel then spoke to the mourners about Noémi's passing. "Grandma taught me many things, but it was her strong sense of optimism and hope, even in the face of evil, that got me through difficult times in my life. If Grandma survived all the atrocities she did, then I knew I could get through whatever I was dealing with. Survival is in my DNA after all! When I was recently feeling depressed and hopeless about disturbing current events, I called Grandma, and she helped restore my hope for the future, telling me, 'Be thankful we live in a country where we can vote and we are free.' She reminded me that she had lived through worse and survived."

Rachel went on to share words from an essay her oldest daughter had recently written: "I want to make sure we all remember the importance of peace and keep it in our hearts." Rachel explained, "My daughter touches on what I feel is the most important lesson to take away from my grandma's life. For a peaceful future, we must continue to tell her story for generations to come. We must teach her messages of love and acceptance, of tolerance and compassion, and always remember to appreciate life."

As Rachel spoke, I looked around at everyone gathered in the synagogue—family and friends who reflected diversity of age, occupation, and spiritual traditions. The tremendous impact Noémi had on the lives of people in our community was evident. Just as Noémi had an incredible gift for uniting people in life, her passing united those who loved and respected her. What we all had in common was our admiration for an extraordinary woman—a special person who touched our lives not only with her story but, most importantly, with her loving presence.

Many of us recognized that Noémi's mission had silently passed into our hands and that it will be up to us to step forward and share her passionate messages. Although our beloved Noémi is no longer with us, I have no doubt that many of us will follow Noémi's tradition of honoring her dear ones by sharing her story. I am also confident that those who read this book will help spread her lessons of hope and healing. Together, we will ensure that Noémi's love lives on.

Diane M. Sue
Bellingham, Washington

About Noémi Ban

Holocaust survivor Noémi Schönberger Ban, born and raised in Hungary, was working as a seventh- and eighth-grade teacher in Budapest at the onset of the Hungarian Revolution of 1956. After escaping Communist Hungary with her husband and two young sons soon after the Revolution, Noémi immigrated to the United States where she learned English, earned a second education degree at the University of Missouri, and began teaching sixth grade at Oakville Elementary School near St. Louis. In 1980, Noémi was named Teacher of the Year in the Mehlville School District and was runner-up for the Missouri Teacher of the Year honor. After retiring in 1982, Noémi and her husband, also a Holocaust survivor, moved to Washington State.

While grieving the loss of her husband, whom she cared for during the five years his health declined due to severe dementia and Parkinson's disease, Noémi was inspired by a speech given by fellow Holocaust survivor and Nobel laureate, Elie Wiesel. Noémi decided

About Noémi Ban

it was time to return to Auschwitz-Birkenau where she had been imprisoned and where most of her family perished. She then dedicated the next three decades of her life to Holocaust education, making over 1,200 presentations throughout the United States and as far away as Hungary and Taiwan. In 2003, Noémi published a youth-oriented Holocaust memoir, *Sharing is Healing.* Her life was also the subject of a 2007 documentary, *My Name is Noémi.*

Noémi received many awards for her public speaking and activism, including an Excellence in Holocaust Education Award, the Washington State Golden Apple Award, the Washington Education Association Human and Civil Rights Award, and induction into the Northwest Women's Hall of Fame. She also received the Americanism Medal from Daughters of the American Revolution (DAR), a prestigious national honor presented to American citizens who have made an outstanding contribution to the nation, and honorary doctorate degrees from both Gonzaga University (1999) and Western Washington University (2013). Noémi proudly raised two sons and has five grandchildren and ten great-grandchildren.

About the Author

Diane M. Sue received her Ph.D. from the University of Michigan, worked as a school psychologist and school counselor for almost thirty years, and has periodically taught adjunct courses in the education and psychology departments at Western Washington University. Diane has been recognized for her professional and volunteer work with children and families, receiving the Washington State School Psychologist of the Year Award and the Western Washington University College of Education Professional Excellence Award. Diane, born in Virginia but raised in California, enjoys her cross-national work conducting conscious aging workshops and her connection with the Humanity Rising global community and with the Center for Spiritual Living. She remains very involved with climate justice work in the Pacific Northwest.

About the Author

Diane first met Noémi in the early 1990s. Diane and Noémi developed a close and lasting friendship, in part because of their common love of teaching and their belief in educating students about kindness, compassion, and resilience. Diane, who incorporates *positive psychology* into her personal life as well as her professional work, embraced Noémi's story and approach to life as a model of many of the character strengths addressed by positive psychologists: bravery; persistence; integrity; vitality; hope; gratitude; love; lifelong learning; perspective and wisdom; active citizenship; humor and playfulness; and a sense of purpose.

Although *Remarkable Resilience: The Life and Legacy of Noémi Ban Beyond the Holocaust* is Diane's first book in this genre, Diane has co-authored psychology textbooks including *Foundations of Counseling and Psychotherapy: Evidence-Based Practices for a Diverse Society* (2008); *Understanding Abnormal Behavior, 12th edition* (2022), and *Essentials of Understanding Abnormal Behavior, 3rd edition* (2017). Writing *Remarkable Resilience* has inspired Diane to take a deeper dive into the socio-political and personal issues brought forward by Noémi's story, as well as the impact that Noémi has had on the lives she touched.

Discussion questions and more details about Noémi's life can be found at Diane's website, LivingWithResilience.com.

www.ingramcontent.com/pod-product-compliance
Lightning Source LLC
Chambersburg PA
CBHW071147130626
46553CB00004B/1556